# UNCLE BEN'S® RICE COOKERY

Rice—The Most Important Food In The World . . . . . . . . . . . . . . . . . 2
Nutrition Information . . . . . . . . . . . . . . . . . . . . . . . . . . . . . . . . . 4
Specialties
   *Unusual things to make with rice* . . . . . . . . . . . . . . . . . . . 13
Salads
   *Add new interest to your meals* . . . . . . . . . . . . . . . . . . . . . 29
Vegetables
   *Frozen or fresh—delicious with rice* . . . . . . . . . . . . . . . . . 44
Side Dishes
   *Start some new traditions at your house* . . . . . . . . . . . . . . 59
Meats
   *Tasty, nourishing combinations of meat and rice* . . . . . . . . . . . . . 76
Poultry
   *Favorite flavors from around the world* . . . . . . . . . . . . . . . . 95
Seafood
   *Expand your culinary horizons with seafood and rice* . . . . . . . . . . 112
Entertaining
   *Memorable meals with the basic goodness of rice* . . . . . . . . . . . . 124
Quick Skillet Dishes
   *Dinner in a hurry; nutritious and flavorful* . . . . . . . . . . . . . . . 142
Make Ahead
   *These recipes give you time with your dinner guests* . . . . . . . . . . . 156
Desserts
   *New ways to serve old-fashioned goodness* . . . . . . . . . . . . . . . 166
Index . . . . . . . . . . . . . . . . . . . . . . . . . . . . . . . . . . . . . . . . . . 175

### ANOTHER BEST-SELLING COOKERY VOLUME FROM H.P. BOOKS

Publisher: Helen Fisher; Editor-in-Chief: Carl Shipman; Editors: Carlene Tejada, Judi Ellingson; Recipe Development: Marian Tripp Communications, Inc.; Art Director: Josh Young; Book Design: Don Burton; Book Assembly: Chris Crosson; Typography: Cindy Coatsworth, Mary Kaye Fisher, Frances Ruiz, Chuck Barlean; Food Stylist: Mable Hoffman; Photography: George deGennaro Studios.

**Published by H.P. Books, P. O. Box 5367, Tucson, AZ 85703**

ISBN: Softcover, 0-912656-78-6; Hardcover, 0-912656-79-4
Library of Congress Catalog Card Number: 77-83278 ©1977 H.P. Books. Printed in U.S.A.

**Cover photo: Paella, see page 129.**

# Rice-The World's Most Important Food

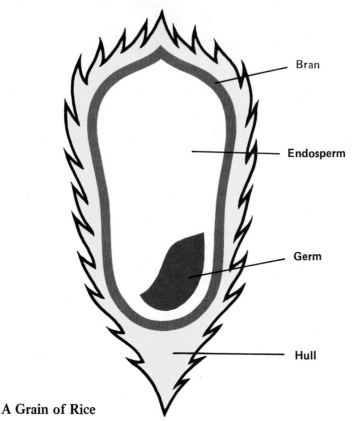

**A Grain of Rice**

*(diagram labels: Bran, Endosperm, Germ, Hull)*

To more than half of the world's population, rice is the basic life-sustaining food, supplying more than 80% of the daily food-energy requirement.

In the Western World we have a great variety of nutritious foods to choose from, including rice prepared in many delicious ways. This book gives you important and interesting facts about rice and how to prepare it. There are 231 tested recipes to help you take advantage of the good basic nutrition offered by rice; its economy and versatility can add to your cookery.

People were cooking and enjoying rice long before they were writing down their favorite recipes—in fact, long before writing was "invented." Rice was cultivated in Southeast Asia about 3,000 years B.C. and from there it spread all over the world, to be embraced by different cultures.

Rice is so easy to prepare and so hospitable to other flavors and ingredients that it has become the basis for many regional and national favorites—each unique and different: Spanish Rice, Arroz con Pollo, New England Rice Pudding, Paella, Rice Pilaf, Chinese Fried Rice, Hoppin' John and New Orleans Rice Calas, just to name a few of the tantalizing variety of delectables you can enjoy with versatile rice. Explore the recipes in this book and give your taste a treat.

## RICE IS A NATURAL FOOD

When you think of rice, you may envision a group of natives working in a flooded rice paddy, planting or harvesting. Rice grown that way has helped nourish the human race since the dawn of history. After harvesting, the hulls were removed from the grains of rice; the rice was cooked and eaten. What could be more natural than that?

If only the outer husk is removed, a grain of rice is still encased in a brownish layer called *bran*. Rice bran is fibrous and chewy, much like wheat bran. A long time ago, people learned to mill both wheat and rice to remove the outer layer of bran.

When rice is milled to remove the bran layer, the result is white grains of rice—the most common kind and the kind preferred all over the world. However, removing the bran also removes some important nutrients if it's done the old-fashioned way. In 1943, Uncle Ben's Foods perfected a way to remove the bran and keep most of the nutrients. The process is called *parboiling.*

# Uncle Ben's Special Parboiling Process

## SEVERAL GOOD REASONS TO USE UNCLE BEN'S® RICE

When preparing the recipes in this book, it makes good sense to use one of the varieties of packaged rice from UNCLE BEN'S® Foods. These recipes were developed and tested with UNCLE BEN'S® Rice products so if you use the UNCLE BEN'S® brand you'll get really good results. Other brands of rice may not work as well in some of these recipes.

That's because the foolproof cooking method for UNCLE BEN'S® CONVERTED® Brand Rice uses more water for the same amount of rice, gives you more servings for the same amount of rice, and produces rice of special flavor and texture with each grain plump and separate—never sticky or lumpy. UNCLE BEN'S® Rice keeps its good taste and appearance longer if you must hold it on the stove or on the table before serving. That's why 80% of the best restaurants in the U.S.A. serve UNCLE BEN'S® Rice.

## UNCLE BEN'S® CONVERTED® BRAND RICE

Much is different about growing and processing rice today, but it's still a natural food, changed very little from the day it was harvested.

The U.S.A. has the most advanced planting and harvesting procedures in the world. Some farmers even sow rice from airplanes. UNCLE BEN'S® Rice is grown in Texas, Arkansas, Louisana and Mississippi and is produced by the most advanced methods.

Before the outer hull and bran are removed, UNCLE BEN'S® CONVERTED® Brand Rice is *parboiled* in a special way, using only water, heat and vacuum. This process takes important nutrients from the outer layers and "locks" them inside the grain of rice. After that, the hull and bran layers are removed but a substantial amount of the B-complex vitamins remain in the endosperm. UNCLE BEN'S® CONVERTED® Brand Rice has *more natural food value* than ordinary white rice because of this special treatment. It retains more than 80% of the natural B-complex vitamins.

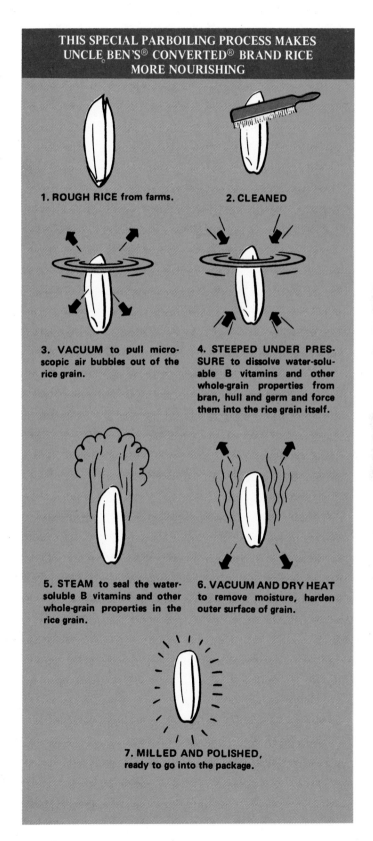

THIS SPECIAL PARBOILING PROCESS MAKES UNCLE BEN'S® CONVERTED® BRAND RICE MORE NOURISHING

1. ROUGH RICE from farms.

2. CLEANED

3. VACUUM to pull microscopic air bubbles out of the rice grain.

4. STEEPED UNDER PRESSURE to dissolve water-soluable B vitamins and other whole-grain properties from bran, hull and germ and force them into the rice grain itself.

5. STEAM to seal the water-soluble B vitamins and other whole-grain properties in the rice grain.

6. VACUUM AND DRY HEAT to remove moisture, harden outer surface of grain.

7. MILLED AND POLISHED, ready to go into the package.

| | UNCLE BEN'S® CONVERTED® Brand Rice | UNCLE BEN'S® QUICK™ Brand Rice | UNCLE BEN'S® Brown Rice | UNCLE BEN'S® Long Grain & Wild Rice | UNCLE BEN'S® Fast Cooking Long Grain & Wild Rice |
|---|---|---|---|---|---|
| Serving Size: | 2/3 cup | 2/3 cup | 2/3 cup | 1/2 cup | 1/2 cup |
| **Per Serving:** | | | | | |
| Calories: | 120 | 110 | 140 | 100 | 100 |
| Protein, g: | 2 | 2 | 3 | 3 | 3 |
| Carbohydrate, g: | 28 | 25 | 29 | 21 | 21 |
| Fat, g: | 0 | 0 | 1 | 0 | 0 |
| **Percentage of U.S. Recommended Daily Allowances (U.S. RDA); per serving** | | | | | |
| Protein | 4 | 2 | 4 | 4 | 4 |
| Vitamin A | * | * | * | * | * |
| Vitamin C | * | * | * | 4 | 4 |
| Thiamine | 10 | 8 | 6 | 6 | 6 |
| Riboflavin | * | * | * | * | * |
| Niacin | 6 | 4 | 6 | 4 | 4 |
| Calcium | * | * | * | * | * |
| Iron | 4 | 4 | 2 | 4 | 4 |

(*) Contains less than 2 percent of the U.S. RDA of these nutrients

## NUTRITIONAL VALUE OF RICE

No single food item should be used as the only ingredient in human nutrition. This applies to rice and all other foods. A balanced diet is essential for good nutrition and health.

Rice supplies a lot of get-up-and-go food energy. For example, one pound of uncooked rice supplies *five times* as much food energy as a pound of uncooked potatoes. It supplies both carbohydrate and protein. Milled white rice has virtually no fat. For complete nutritional data on several UNCLE BEN'S® Rice products, see the table on this page.

## WHAT KIND OF RICE IS BEST?

Three distinct kinds of rice are grown in the world, described as long-grain, medium-grain and short-grain. Many rice-growing countries produce only one type. In the United States, all three kinds are grown.

Another delicious food is wild rice. Technically, this is not rice; it belongs to a different plant family. It grows on native grasses in marshes and wetlands of Minnesota and Canada. It has been harvested for centuries by American Indians, in canoes, using simple methods. A law requires use of the same hand-harvesting methods today because this leaves some of the grains in the lakes. It is necessary to leave some seeds for the next crop.

Although there are some regional and ethnic preferences for different types of rice, long-grain rice is preferred by most people in the Western World for use in general cooking. When cooked, the grains are plump and separate; they do not stick together; they hold their shape and have an excellent flavor. Even though other kinds of rice are grown in the U.S.A., UNCLE BEN'S® is long-grain rice only.

Medium-grain and short-grain rice grains tend to stick together when cooked. They become soft and mushy if overcooked, held on the stove or table before serving, or refrigerated and then reheated.

## WHY YOU SHOULD NEVER WASH RICE

People usually wash foods like field-grown vegetables before cooking. The idea is to wash away dirt, leaves and things like that.

Rice out of the package does not need washing. It has already been washed, cleaned, milled to remove the outer layers and packaged under strict sanitary conditions.

Vitamins and nutrients are water-soluble.

Some people wash rice three times! Once before cooking—out goes some food value. Then they cook it in too much water and throw away the excess water when finished. This amounts to washing it in hot water for a rather long time—out goes food value. After that, some dedicated rice-washers even rinse the cooked rice—and out goes still more food value.

Please don't wash UNCLE BEN'S® Rice even once!

## YOU CAN COOK RICE WITH CONFIDENCE

For thousands of years, people have been cooking rice successfully, three times a day. Sometimes this is done under primitive or adverse conditions—outdoors; over a flickering hard-to-control fire; in a makeshift pot of some kind. Isn't it surprising that some cooks in a modern kitchen say, "My Goodness, I just can't cook rice."

You can cook rice successfully every time, if you do two simple things. Use UNCLE BEN'S® because it is long-grain rice, specially processed to assure success. Follow the cooking instructions on the package, and in this book, *exactly* until it becomes second nature. It's so simple, you'll end up saying, "My Goodness, cooking perfect rice is easy!"

**PREPARE PERFECT RICE EVERY TIME USING UNCLE BEN'S® CONVERTED® BRAND RICE**

BASIC RECIPE: (Makes 3 - 4 cups cooked rice or 5 to 6 2/3-cup servings).

1. Bring 2-1/2 cups water to a boil.

2. Stir in 1 cup rice, 1 teaspoon salt and if desired, 1 tablespoon butter or margarine.

3. Cover tightly and simmer 20 minutes.

4. Remove from heat. Let stand covered until all water is absorbed, about 5 minutes.

**For SOFTER rice use MORE water and simmer LONGER.**
**For FIRMER rice use LESS water and simmer for a SHORTER time.**

**UNCLE BEN'S® CONVERTED® Brand Rice**

is long-grain milled white rice specially parboiled to retain many of the natural nutrients. The grains remain separate and fluffy after cooking, even if kept awhile before serving. Cooks in 25 minutes.

**UNCLE BEN'S® QUICK™ Brand Rice**

is UNCLE BEN'S® CONVERTED® Brand Rice that has been precooked and then dehydrated before packaging. It can be prepared at home in only 5 minutes, but has the same flavor, texture and advantages as UNCLE BEN'S® CONVERTED® Brand Rice.

**UNCLE BEN'S® LONG GRAIN & WILD RICE**

is a blend of long-grain, wild rice and seasonings. Wild rice is a flavorful wild grass, native to northern Minnesota and Canada, harvested in the same way American Indians have done for centuries. This is a unique convenience product with a delicious blend of 23 herbs, seasonings and spices already in the package. The long-grain rice is specially parboiled to retain nutrition, just the same as UNCLE BEN'S® CONVERTED® Brand Rice. Makes a delicious flavor treat in only 25 minutes cooking time.

**UNCLE BEN'S® FAST COOKING LONG GRAIN & WILD RICE**

is similar to UNCLE BEN'S® LONG GRAIN & WILD RICE except that it has been precooked and dehydrated before packaging to give you the convenience of 5-minute preparation. Also, the herbs and spices are different, so you have a choice of two exciting long-grain and wild-rice dishes.

**UNCLE BEN'S® BROWN RICE**

is long-grain rice with only the outer hull removed in processing. It retains many of the natural vitamins and minerals and has a nut-like flavor with a chewy texture. Due to the special parboiling process, it has excellent keeping qualities and remains separate and non-sticky when cooked. Cooks in about 50 minutes.

  The recipes in this book use 5 different kinds of UNCLE BEN'S® Rice—not all in the same recipe, of course. Both types of Long Grain & Wild Rice contain seasoning packets which you'll use in some recipes.

### REHEATING COOKED RICE

Many good cooks like to make a larger amount of a favorite dish, serve part of it and freeze the remainder or store it in the refrigerator for later use. Just be sure it is frozen or refrigerated promptly. Thrifty cooks don't throw leftovers away.

UNCLE BEN'S® rice products and prepared dishes made with rice can be frozen or refrigerated and then reheated on the stove or in the oven just by adding a little water to the container.

Of course you can also enjoy the convenience of reheating in a microwave oven. Experience and the manufacturer's instructions are the best guide to using your brand of microwave oven. The best rule is, *don't overcook.* Heat for a short time, check, and heat some more if necessary. Use a container suitable for your microwave oven and add a few drops of water if needed to retain that moist just-cooked appearance and texture.

You'll find that the special processing given

Clockwise from top: UNCLE BEN'S® CONVERTED® Brand Rice, UNCLE BEN'S® Long Grain & Wild Rice, UNCLE BEN'S® Brown Rice and UNCLE BEN'S® QUICK™ Brand Rice

UNCLE BEN'S® rice makes it superior for storing and reheating.

## COOKING RICE IN YOUR MICROWAVE OVEN

There is no special advantage in cooking rice from the package in your microwave. It doesn't cook any faster than on your stove and you have to open the microwave oven door several times to stir the rice.

On the other hand, there is no reason not to cook rice in your microwave if you want to. Instructions for UNCLE BEN'S® Rice products are included in this book. Because different brands of microwave ovens cook differently, you may have to experiment a bit to get the timing and power setting just right. Remember, it's better to undercook and then cook more than it is to overcook and be sorry.

## COOKING RICE IN YOUR ELECTRIC SLOW COOKER

You can cook rice in a slow cooker, but it doesn't come out with the same texture you will get by using other cooking methods. It's largely a matter of personal taste or convenience. Instructions for cooking rice in an electric slow cooker are also included in this book.

You should know that a leading manufacturer of electric slow cookers recommends *only* UNCLE BEN'S® Rice products because they do very well under the long slow cooking procedure. Other types of rice without UNCLE BEN'S® special processing may turn out sticky or mushy.

Some electric slow-cooker recipes suggest adding rice near the end of the cooking period rather than leaving it in from the beginning. If you find a recipe that uses this method, the rice is more likely to resemble rice cooked on top of the stove.

---

When the recipes in this book call for a large skillet, use a skillet that is 12-inches wide. Of course, you may use a larger skillet. It's possible to use a smaller skillet for some of the recipes, but because rice absorbs liquid as it cooks and therefore expands, always use a pan large enough to prevent an overflow.

When the recipes in this book call for a large saucepan, use a 2-quart saucepan.

---

## COOKING METHODS FOR UNCLE BEN'S® QUICK™ BRAND RICE

### Package Directions
1. Stir together in saucepan, 2 cups rice, 1-2/3 cups water, 1/2 teaspoon salt and 1 tablespoon butter or margarine.
2. Bring to a vigorous boil.
3. Cover and simmer until all water is absorbed, about 5 minutes.

### Excess Water
1. Bring 1 quart water and 1-1/2 teaspoons salt to a boil.
2. Stir in 2 cups rice. Bring back to a boil.
3. Cover and remove from heat. Let stand about 10 minutes.
4. Drain well. Fold in 1 tablespoon butter or margarine.

### Microwave Oven
1. Stir together in 1-1/2 quart non-metallic casserole, 2 cups rice, 1-2/3 cups water, 1/2 teaspoon salt and 1 tablespoon butter.
2. Cover and cook at HIGH setting until all water is absorbed, about 8 to 10 minutes.

### Grill or Campfire
1. Place in disposable aluminum pan or pouch made from heavy-duty aluminum foil, 2 cups rice, 1-2/3 cups water, 1/2 teaspoon salt and 1 tablespoon butter or margarine. Stir well.
2. Cover pan with foil or seal pouch by folding edges over.
3. Place on grill and cook until all liquid is absorbed. The time will depend on distance from heat. On a grill 5 inches above heat, the cooking time is approximately 20 minutes.

## Package Directions

1. Bring 2-1/2 cups water to a boil in saucepan.
2. Stir in 1 cup rice, 1 teaspoon salt and if desired, 1 table-spoon butter or margarine.
3. Cover tightly and simmer 20 minutes.
4. Remove from heat. Let stand covered until all water is absorbed, about 5 minutes.

## Oven

1. Place 1 cup rice in a 1-1/2 quart casserole.
2. Bring 2-1/4 cups water, 1 tea-spoon salt and, if desired, 1 tablespoon butter or marga-rine to a boil in saucepan.
3. Pour over rice. Stir well.
4. Cover and bake in 350°F (177°C) oven until water is absorbed, about 30 to 35 minutes.

## Excess Water

1. Bring 1-1/2 to 2 quarts water and 1 tablespoon salt to a boil.
2. Stir in 1 cup rice.
3. Boil gently 20 to 25 minutes or until rice is tender.
4. Drain. Fold in 1 tablespoon butter or margarine, if desired.

## Skillet (Regular or Electric)

1. Melt 1 tablespoon butter or margarine in a skillet.
2. Add 1 cup rice and stir until coated with butter.
3. Stir in 2-1/2 cups water and 1 teaspoon salt. Bring to a boil.
4. Cover and simmer until liquid is absorbed, about 25 minutes.

## Wok (Regular or Electric)

1. Heat 1 tablespoon cooking oil, butter or margarine in wok over low heat.
2. Add 1 cup rice and stir until coated with oil
3. Stir in 2-1/4 cups water and 1 teaspoon salt. Bring to a boil.
4. Cover and simmer until water is absorbed, about 20 to 25 minutes.

## Double Boiler

1. Bring 2-1/4 cups water to a boil in top section of double boiler.
2. Stir in 1 cup rice, 1 teaspoon salt and, if desired, 1 table-spoon butter or margarine.
3. Place over gently boiling water in bottom section of double boiler.
4. Cover and cook until all water is absorbed, about 35 minutes.

## Microwave Oven

1. Combine 1 cup rice, 2-1/2 cups water, 1 teaspoon salt and, if desired, 1 tablespoon butter or margarine in a 2-quart non-metallic casserole. Stir well.
2. Cover and cook in microwave oven at HIGH setting about 20 minutes, stirring occasionally.
3. Remove from oven. Let stand until all liquid is absorbed, about 5 minutes.

## Electric Slow Cooker

1. Combine 1 cup rice, 2-1/2 cups water, 1 teaspoon salt and, if desired, 1 tablespoon butter or margarine in slow cooker. Stir well.
2. Cover and cook on HIGH heat until water is absorbed, about 1-1/2 to 2 hours.

## Presoak

1. Combine 1 cup rice, 2-1/2 cups water and 1 teaspoon salt in saucepan.
2. Cover and place in refrigerator overnight or at least 2 hours.
3. Add butter or margarine if desired. Bring to a boil.
4. Cover and simmer until water is absorbed, about 15 minutes.

## Rice Cookers

There are several types of rice cookers on the market which cook rice by either a steam or dry heat method. The directions with many of these cookers are for cooking a regular milled rice rather than a parboiled rice like UNCLE BEN'S® CONVERTED® Brand Rice. Cookers vary and you may need to adjust the amount of water to obtain the desired rice texture. The following will serve as a *guide only* for cooking UNCLE BEN'S® CON-VERTED® Brand Rice in the various types of cookers:

*Automatic Steam Type*
Use about 2 cups water to 1 cup of rice in inner pan and about 1/2 cup water in outer pot. Follow cooker manufacturers' direc-tions for cooking rice. When cooker shuts off, let rice stand covered in cooker about 5 minutes or until all water is absorbed.

*Automatic Direct Heat Type*
Use amount of ingredients speci-fied on package and follow man-ufacturers' directions for turning cooker on. Cook only until most of water is absorbed, about 25 minutes, then manually turn off cooker. Let stand covered in cooker until all water is absorbed, about 5 minutes.

*Top-of-Stove Rice Steamers*
Use about 2 cups water to 1 cup rice in inner pan. Cook according to steamer manufacturers' direc-tions until all water is absorbed, about 25 minutes.

## COOKING METHODS FOR UNCLE BEN'S® FAST COOKING LONG GRAIN & WILD RICE

**Package Directions**
1. Measure 2 cups water and 2 tablespoons butter or margarine into saucepan.
2. Stir in contents of both packets from package. Bring to a vigorous boil.
3. Cover and simmer until all water is absorbed, about 5 utes.

**Microwave Oven**
1. Combine contents of both packets from package, 2 cups water and 2 tablespoons butter or margarine in a 1-1/2 quart non-metallic casserole.
2. Cover and cook at high setting until all liquid is absorbed, about 8 to 10 minutes.

## COOKING METHODS FOR UNCLE BEN'S® LONG GRAIN & WILD RICE

**Package Directions**
1. Measure 2-1/2 cups water and 1 tablespoon butter or margarine in saucepan.
2. Stir in contents of both packets in package. Bring to a boil.
3. Cover tightly and cook over low heat until all water is absorbed, about 25 minutes.

**Oven**
1. Place contents of both packets in package in a 1-1/2 quart casserole.
2. Bring 2-1/4 cups water and 1 tablespoon butter or margarine to a boil in saucepan.
3. Pour over rice mixture. Stir well.
4. Cover and bake in 350°F (177°C) oven until water is absorbed, about 35 to 40 minutes.

**Microwave Oven**
1. Combine contents of both packets in package, 2-1/2 cups water and 1 tablespoon butter or margarine in 2-quart non-metallic casserole.
2. Cover and cook at HIGH setting about 20 minutes, stirring occasionally.
3. Remove from oven. Let stand covered until liquid is absorbed, about 5 to 10 minutes.

## COOKING METHODS FOR UNCLE BEN'S® BROWN RICE

**Package Directions**
1. Bring 2-2/3 cups water to a boil in saucepan.
2. Stir in 1 cup rice, 1 teaspoon salt and 1 tablespoon butter.
3. Cover tightly and cook over low heat until all water is absorbed, about 50 minutes.

**Electric Slow Cooker**
1. Rub 1 tablespoon butter or margarine over bottom and up sides of slow cooker.
2. Add 1 cup rice, 2-2/3 cups water and 1 teaspoon salt.
3. Cover and cook on HIGH heat until all liquid is absorbed, about 3 hours.

| PROBLEM | CAUSE | CURE |
|---|---|---|
| Too firm | Not enough liquid | Add more liquid and cook longer |
| | Too large a pan used causing excessive evaporation of water | Use smaller size pan |
| Too soft | Too much liquid | Use less liquid and cook for shorter time |
| | Cooked too long | Reduce cooking time |
| Grains stick together | Stirring during cooking | Avoid stirring during cooking and set-aside time |
| | Cooked too long | Reduce cooking time |
| | Holding large quantity in pan after liquid is absorbed | When preparing two or more cups, immediately transfer the cooked rice to serving dish |
| Liquid not absorbed in time given in directions | Incorrect proportions used | Measure accurately |
| | Heat too low | Use higher heat |
| Not as dry as desired | Cooking method used may not result in dry rice | Remove cover after cooking and leave on very low heat for 4 to 5 minutes |
| Sticks to bottom of pan | Cooked too long | Reduce cooking time |
| | Heat too high | Use lower heat |
| Does not get soft when cooked in milk | Type of rice. Parboiled rice does not become soft when cooked in milk. | Precook the rice in water before adding milk |
| Becomes hard and chalky when refrigerated | Type of rice. Any long grain variety of rice will become firm when refrigerated due to a change in starch called *retrogradation.* | Reheat, adding a small amount of water. Cook rice for refrigerated desserts in excess water until very soft to help retard the firming process |
| "Pops" when cooked in butter, margarine or oil | Parboiled rice will pop if heat is too high | Cook over low heat, stirring constantly |
| Liquid foams out of pan | Heat too high | Reduce heat |
| | Pan size too small | Use larger pan |
| Gritty texture | Removing cover often during cooking of a regular milled white rice | Avoid removing lid until near end of cooking time |

## CONVERSION TO METRIC MEASURE

| WHEN YOU KNOW | SYMBOL | MULTIPLY BY | TO FIND | SYMBOL |
|---|---|---|---|---|
| teaspoons | tsp | 5 | milliliters | ml |
| tablespoons | tbsp | 15 | milliliters | ml |
| fluid ounces | fl oz | 30 | milliliters | ml |
| cups | c | 0.24 | liters | l |
| pints | pt | 0.47 | liters | l |
| quarts | qt | 0.95 | liters | l |
| ounces | oz | 28 | grams | g |
| pounds | lb | 0.45 | kilograms | kg |
| Fahrenheit | °F | 5/9 (after subtracting 32) | Celsius | C |
| inches | in | 2.54 | centimeters | cm |
| feet | ft | 30.5 | centimeters | cm |

## LIQUID MEASURE TO MILLILITERS

| | | |
|---|---|---|
| 1/4 teaspoon | = | 1.25 milliliters |
| 1/2 teaspoon | = | 2.5 milliliters |
| 3/4 teaspoon | = | 3.75 milliliters |
| 1 teaspoon | = | 5 milliliters |
| 1-1/4 teaspoons | = | 6.25 milliliters |
| 1-1/2 teaspoons | = | 7.5 milliliters |
| 1-3/4 teaspoons | = | 8.75 milliliters |
| 2 teaspoons | = | 10 milliliters |
| 1 tablespoon | = | 15 milliliters |
| 2 tablespoons | = | 30 milliliters |

## LIQUID MEASURE TO LITERS

| | | |
|---|---|---|
| 1/4 cup | = | 0.06 liters |
| 1/2 cup | = | 0.12 liters |
| 3/4 cup | = | 0.18 liters |
| 1 cup | = | 0.24 liters |
| 1-1/4 cups | = | 0.3 liters |
| 1-1/2 cups | = | 0.36 liters |
| 2 cups | = | 0.48 liters |
| 2-1/2 cups | = | 0.6 liters |
| 3 cups | = | 0.72 liters |
| 3-1/2 cups | = | 0.84 liters |
| 4 cups | = | 0.96 liters |
| 4-1/2 cups | = | 1.08 liters |
| 5 cups | = | 1.2 liters |
| 5-1/2 cups | = | 1.32 liters |

## FAHRENHEIT TO CELSIUS

| F | C |
|---|---|
| 200° | 93° |
| 225° | 107° |
| 250° | 121° |
| 275° | 135° |
| 300° | 149° |
| 325° | 163° |
| 350° | 177° |
| 375° | 191° |
| 400° | 205° |
| 425° | 218° |
| 450° | 232° |
| 475° | 246° |
| 500° | 260° |

# Specialties

A cup or so of one of UNCLE BEN'S® Rice products can be the basis for a hearty bowl of soup, a tasty loaf of bread, crispy fritters or talk-of-the-town appetizers. In this section you'll find a new recipe for Calas, a New Orleans rice-fritter brunch treat, dipped in sugar and shredded orange peel.

Send the family breadwinner off tomorrow with a piece of Apricot-Yogurt Bread in his lunch box. After the game or theater, you and your guests can enjoy spicy Taco Soup. And it's easy to prepare, too. Check the recipes in this section and see for yourself how versatile UNCLE BEN'S® Rice is.

### Soup & Salad Spread
   Avocado Salad
* Cioppino
   Hot Sourdough Bread
   Assorted Cheeses
   Apple Tart

### New Orleans Brunch
   Broiled Grapefruit Halves
   Mushroom Omelet
   Grilled Ham Slices
   Asparagus Almondine
* Calas

### Holiday Party
* Wild Rice Mushrooms
* Clams Mornay
* Chili Salad in Cherry Tomatoes
   Guacamole Dip
   Assorted Dippers
   Taco Chips
   Mixed Nuts

### Come for Coffee
   Chilled Fresh Fruit
* Apricot-Yogurt Bread
   Pecan Coffee Cake
   Butter
   Selection of Coffees

### Saturday Patio Get-Together
* California-Style Beef Stew
   Crusty French Bread
   Big Salad Bowl
   Fresh Fruit with Sherbet
   Cookies

### Monday Night Football
   Guacamole
   Corn Chips
* Taco Soup
   Cole Slaw
   Cheddar Cheese & Breads
   Butterscotch Bars

*These recipes are in this section.*

# Cioppino

*Also known as San Francisco Fish Stew.*

1-1/2 lbs. fish fillets, fresh or frozen
2 tablespoons olive oil
2 tablespoons butter or margarine
1-1/2 cups sliced onion
2 cloves garlic, minced
1 (1-lb. 12-oz.) can tomatoes
1 (8-oz.) can tomato sauce
1 cup dry white wine
1 cup water
2 tablespoons chopped parsley
1-1/2 teaspoons salt
1-1/2 teaspoons basil

1/2 teaspoon oregano
1 lb. fresh shrimp, cleaned and deveined,
   with tails on, or 1 (4-1/2-oz.) can shrimp,
   drained and rinsed
12 to 16 fresh clams, well washed or
   1 (8-oz.) can minced clams
3 cups UNCLE BEN'S® QUICK™
   Brand Rice
2-1/3 cups water
3/4 teaspoon salt
1-1/2 tablespoons butter or margarine

Thaw fish, if frozen. In a large skillet, combine oil and butter or margarine. Add onion and garlic. Cook 2 minutes. Add tomatoes, tomato sauce, wine, water, parsley, salt, basil and oregano. Cover. Simmer to blend flavors, about 30 minutes. Cut fish into 1-inch to 1-1/2-inch chunks. Add to tomato mixture. Cover. Simmer about 20 minutes. Add shrimp and clams. Cover and simmer until fish flakes easily, shrimp are tender and clams open. Cook rice with 2-1/3 cups water, 3/4 teaspoon salt and 1-1/2 tablespoons butter or margarine according to package directions. Serve stew in bowls over hot cooked rice. Makes 8 servings.

# Eggs-Carmen Brunch

*Saucy eggs on cheese-flavored Spanish-style rice.*

6 slices bacon, diced
1 (6-1/4-oz.) pkg. UNCLE BEN'S® Fast
   Cooking Long Grain & Wild Rice
1 (1-lb.) can stewed tomatoes, undrained
1/4 teaspoon basil
1/2 cup shredded Cheddar cheese

1/4 cup chopped pitted ripe olives
2/3 cup dairy sour cream
1/8 teaspoon Dijon mustard
4 large eggs
Chopped fresh parsley, if desired

Preheat oven to 350°F (177°C). Lightly butter or oil 4 individual casseroles or ramekins. In a large skillet, sauté bacon over low heat until lightly browned, stirring often; do not drain. Add contents of rice and seasoning packets, tomatoes and basil. Break up large tomato pieces. Bring to a boil; stir. Reduce heat and cover. Simmer 5 minutes. Remove from heat. Stir in cheese, olives and 1/2 cup of the sour cream. Spoon into prepared individual casseroles or ramekins. With back of tablespoon make a deep indentation in center of each portion. Bake 15 minutes. Combine remaining sour cream and mustard. Remove casseroles from oven. Turn 1 egg into indentation in each rice portion. Spoon a dollop of sour cream-mustard mixture on each yolk. Return to oven. Continue baking until egg whites are set, but yolks still soft, 6 to 10 minutes. Garnish eggs with parsley, if desired, and serve at once. Makes 4 servings.

# Hearty Polish Soup

*Serve with crusty bread and a crisp green salad.*

4 slices bacon, diced
3 medium onions, sliced
1/2-lb. beef, cut in 1/2-in. cubes
1/2-lb. pork, cut in 1/2-in. cubes
1 tablespoon caraway seeds
2 teaspoons seasoned salt
1 teaspoon garlic powder
1/2 teaspoon paprika

1/4 teaspoon pepper
2 beef-bouillon cubes, crushed
8 cups water
1/2 cup UNCLE BEN'S® CONVERTED®
   Brand Rice
1 lb. smoked Polish sausage, sliced
1 medium tomato, chopped
Garlic croutons

In a Dutch oven, fry bacon until crisp. Remove bacon bits; drain on paper toweling. Pour off all but 2 tablespoons bacon drippings. Add onions, beef and pork. Cook until onion is tender, stirring often. Add caraway seeds, seasoned salt, garlic powder, paprika, pepper, bouillon cubes and 2 cups of the water. Cover. Cook 1-1/2 hours stirring frequently. Add remaining water, rice, sausage and tomato. Bring to a boil and cover. Simmer until beef and pork are tender, about 25 minutes. Serve topped with bacon bits and croutons. Makes 10 servings.

# Rice & Rye Bread

*You'll enjoy this mellow, nutritious bread.*

1 (6-oz.) pkg. UNCLE BEN'S®
   Long Grain & Wild Rice
2-1/2 cups water
1 tablespoon butter or margarine
2 cups all-purpose flour
2 (1/4-oz.) pkgs. active dry yeast
2 tablespoons caraway seeds

1 tablespoon salt
2 cups milk
1/4 cup vegetable oil
1/4 cup light molasses
1 egg, slightly beaten
3 cups rye flour
2 cups all-purpose flour

Butter two 8-1/2" x 4-1/2" loaf pans. Lightly butter a large bowl for rising of dough. Cook contents of rice and seasoning packets with water and butter or margarine according to package directions. Let cool while preparing other ingredients. Combine 2 cups all-purpose flour, yeast, caraway seeds and salt in electric-mixer bowl; stir. Combine milk and vegetable oil. Heat until mixture measures 130°F (54°C) on a cooking thermometer. Measure 1-1/2 cups cooked rice. Use remaining rice another time. Add the 1-1/2 cups rice, molasses, egg and milk-oil mixture to flour mixture. With electric mixer, beat slowly until ingredients are moistened, then beat at medium speed 3 minutes. With a wooden spoon, stir in rye flour and 2 cups all-purpose flour as needed to make a stiff dough. Knead on lightly floured board until dough is smooth, about 2 minutes. Place dough in lightly buttered bowl; turn once to butter the top. Cover and let rise in warm place until doubled in size, about 45 minutes. Punch down and form into 2 loaves. Place in buttered loaf pans. Let rise in warm place until doubled in size, 30 to 40 minutes. Bake at 350°F (177°C) until browned, about 40 minutes. Baked loaves should sound hollow when tapped on top crust. Remove from pans and cool on racks. Makes 2 loaves.

# Chili Salad in Cherry Tomatoes

*Stuff dainty cherry tomatoes with zesty rice.*

1/2 cup UNCLE BEN'S® CONVERTED®
  Brand Rice
1-1/3 cups water
1/2 teaspoon salt
1/2 tablespoon butter or margarine
1/2 cup dairy sour cream
1/2 cup mayonnaise

1/4 teaspoon salt
1 (4-oz.) can chopped green chilies,
  drained
1 (3-1/2-oz.) can pitted ripe olives,
  drained and chopped
3 green onions, chopped
7 to 8 dozen cherry tomatoes

Cook rice with water, 1/2 teaspoon salt and butter or margarine according to package directions for half the basic recipe. Cover and chill well. Add sour cream, mayonnaise and salt. Mix well. Add green chilies, olives and green onions; mix. Chill until serving time. Cut off top 1/3 of each cherry tomato. Remove seeds and pulp with a small spoon. Drain insides of tomatoes well. Fill each tomato with salad, using about a rounded teaspoonful of salad for each one, depending on size of tomato. Makes about 3 cups of salad or enough for 7 to 8 dozen appetizers.

# Stuffed Grape Leaves

*Delectable, crowd-pleasing appetizers.*

3 large onions, chopped
1/2 cup vegetable oil
1 (6-oz.) pkg. UNCLE BEN'S®
  Long Grain & Wild Rice
1 (8-oz.) can tomato sauce
1-1/2 cups water
2 teaspoons salt

1/4 teaspoon ground pepper
1-1/2 cups fresh parsley, minced
2 tablespoons lemon juice
1 (16-oz.) jar grape leaves
2 cups water
Parsley for garnish
Lemon wedges for garnish

Preheat oven to 350°F (177°C). In a large skillet, cook onions in vegetable oil until golden. Stir in contents of rice and seasoning packets, tomato sauce and water. Bring to a boil. Cover tightly. Cook over low heat until all liquid is absorbed, about 25 minutes. Stir in salt, pepper, parsley and lemon juice. Rinse grape leaves under cold water; dry thoroughly. Place leaves rib side down. Place a rounded teaspoonful of filling in center of each leaf. Fold both sides over to center. Fold over one end and roll up. Arrange in a 2-quart casserole, seam side down. Add 2 cups water. Weight down stuffed leaves with an oven-proof plate. Bake 45 minutes. Refrigerate until chilled, still weighted down. Serve cold with parsley and lemon wedges. Makes 60 to 70 appetizers.

Chili Salad in Cherry Tomatoes
Stuffed Grape Leaves

# Calas

*Our editors love these orange-flavored brunch treats.*

2 cups UNCLE BEN'S® QUICK™
  Brand Rice
1-2/3 cups water
1/2 teaspoon salt
1 tablespoon butter or margarine
2 eggs
1/4 cup half and half

2 tablespoons sugar
2 teaspoons grated orange peel
2 cups prepared biscuit mix
2 to 3 cups vegetable oil
2/3 cup sugar
2 teaspoons grated orange peel

Cook rice with water, salt and butter or margarine according to package directions. Cool. Beat eggs, half and half and 2 tablespoons sugar together. Stir in rice and 2 teaspoons orange peel. Stir in biscuit mix until all dry particles are moistened. Pour about 1 inch of oil into a small saucepan and heat to 350°F (176°C) on a cooking thermometer. Drop mixture by rounded tablespoons into hot oil. Cook 3 to 4 calas at a time for 4 to 5 minutes, turning to lightly brown both sides. Remove from hot oil with slotted spoon, draining slightly. Combine 2/3 cup of sugar and remaining 2 teaspoons orange peel. Drop calas into orange sugar and toss lightly to coat evenly. Remove and keep warm until ready to serve. Makes about 3 dozen.

# Tomato-Rice Quiche

*A memorable variation—and it needs no pastry crust!*

2 tablespoons fine corn-flake crumbs
1 cup UNCLE BEN'S® CONVERTED®
  Brand Rice
2-1/2 cups water
1 teaspoon salt
1 tablespoon butter or margarine
1/4-lb. bacon, diced
1 medium onion, chopped

1 medium green pepper, chopped
1 medium tomato, chopped
1-1/2 cups shredded Swiss cheese
2 eggs
1/2 cup half and half
1 tablespoon flour
1-1/2 teaspoons salt

Preheat oven to 325°F (163°C). Generously butter a 10-inch pie pan. Sprinkle bottom and sides with corn-flake crumbs to coat evenly. Cook rice with water, 1 teaspoon salt and butter or margarine according to package directions; cool. Press cooked rice over bottom and up sides of corn-flake-lined pan, making an even layer. Fry bacon until crisp; remove and drain. Add onion to bacon drippings. Cook until tender, but not brown. Add green pepper and tomato. Cook, stirring, until heated through. Layer cheese, bacon and vegetable mixture in rice shell, making 2 layers of each. In a small bowl, beat eggs with half and half, flour and 1-1/2 teaspoons salt until smooth. Carefully pour mixture over layered filling. Bake until mixture is set, about 35 minutes. Remove from oven. Let stand about 15 minutes before cutting into wedges. Makes 6 servings.

# Wild Rice Mushrooms

*Easy and elegant.*

1 cup chopped onions
3 tablespoons butter
2-1/2 cups chicken broth
1 (6-oz.) pkg. UNCLE BEN'S®
    Long Grain & Wild Rice
1/2 cup minced cooked ham

3 cloves garlic, minced
1/2 cup butter
4 dozen 2-in.-wide fresh mushrooms,
    stems removed
2 tablespoons lemon juice
Salt and pepper to taste

In a large saucepan, cook onions in 3 tablespoons melted butter until soft. Stir in broth, contents of rice and seasoning packets. Bring to a boil. Cover tightly. Cook over moderate heat until water is absorbed, about 25 minutes. Add ham and set aside. In a large skillet, cook garlic in 1/2 cup butter until golden. Add mushrooms and lemon juice. Cook over moderate heat for 4 to 5 minutes. Spoon rice mixture into mushrooms. Serve hot. Heat under broiler, if necessary. Makes 4 dozen appetizers.

# Natural-Goodness Bread

*A crunchy, good and good-for-you bread treat.*

1 cup water
1 cup UNCLE BEN'S® QUICK™
    Brand Rice
1 cup flour
2 (1/4-oz.) pkgs. active dry yeast
1/4 cup sugar
1 tablespoon salt

1-1/2 cups buttermilk
1/4 cup vegetable oil
1 cup seedless raisins
1/2 cup shelled sunflower seeds
1/4 cup toasted sesame seeds
3-1/2 to 4 cups flour

Butter two 9" x 5" loaf pans. Lightly butter a large bowl for rising of dough. Bring water to a boil. Remove from heat; stir in rice. Cover. Let stand while preparing other ingredients. Combine 1 cup flour, yeast, sugar and salt in electric-mixer bowl. Mix well. Heat buttermilk and vegetable oil until warm, 130°F (54°C). Add buttermilk-oil mixture to flour mixture; blend at low speed until dry ingredients are moistened. Beat at medium speed 5 minutes. Stir in rice-water mixture, raisins, sunflower seeds, sesame seeds and enough flour to make an easy-to-handle dough. Knead on lightly floured surface until smooth and elastic, about 5 minutes. Place in buttered bowl; turn once to butter top. Cover. Let rise in warm place until light and doubled in size, about 1 hour. Punch down dough. Cut in half. Shape into 2 loaves. Place in buttered loaf pans and cover. Let rise in warm place until doubled in size, about 1 hour. Bake at 375°F (191°C) until done, 35 to 50 minutes. Remove from pans and cool on rack. Makes 2 loaves.

# Florentine Rice Roll

*Impressive in appearance and flavor.*

1/2 cup UNCLE BEN'S® CONVERTED®
  Brand Rice
1-1/3 cups water
1/2 teaspoon salt
1/2 tablespoon butter or margarine
1/4 cup butter or margarine
1/3 cup flour

1/2 teaspoon salt
2 cups milk
4 eggs, separated
1 tablespoon Dijon mustard
Spinach-Mushroom Filling, see below
Pimiento for garnish

*Spinach-Mushroom Filling:*

2 cups chopped fresh mushrooms
3/4 cup chopped onion
2 tablespoons butter or margarine
1 (10-oz.) pkg. frozen chopped spinach,
  thawed
1/2 cup chopped ham

2 (3-oz.) pkgs. cream cheese,
  room temperature
1 tablespoon Dijon mustard
1/2 teaspoon salt
1/4 teaspoon ground nutmeg

Preheat oven to 400°F (205°C). Oil a 15" x 10" x 1" baking pan; line with wax paper and oil again. Coat lightly with flour. Cook rice with water, 1/2 teaspoon salt and 1/2 tablespoon butter or margarine according to package directions for half the basic recipe. In a large saucepan, melt 1/4 cup butter or margarine. Blend in flour and 1/2 teaspoon salt. Add milk. Cook, stirring constantly, until thickened. Beat egg yolks slightly. Add a small amount of hot flour-milk mixture to beaten egg yolks, beating constantly. Return to pan. Cook 1 minute, stirring constantly. Stir in cooked rice and mustard. Beat egg whites until they hold soft peaks. Carefully fold into rice mixture. Pour into prepared pan and spread evenly. Bake until puffed and lightly browned, about 20 minutes. Turn out on towel. Remove wax paper. Spread evenly with Spinach-Mushroom Filling to within 1 inch of 1 lengthwise edge. Roll up, starting on the long side with filling spread to edge. Place on serving platter. Cut into 1 to 1-1/4-inch slices. Garnish slices with pimiento. Makes 12 to 14 appetizer servings.

**Spinach-Mushroom Filling:**

In a large saucepan, cook mushrooms and onion slowly in butter or margarine until tender. Stir in spinach. Cook until spinach is tender and moisture evaporates. Add ham, cream cheese, mustard, salt and nutmeg. Stir until evenly blended. Makes filling for 1 roll.

**Variation:**

For best results, prepare and fill rice roll just before serving. However, with some loss in quality the roll can be prepared ahead of time and reheated as follows: Cool roll; do not cut. Wrap securely in aluminum foil. Refrigerate until ready to serve. To reheat, place wrapped roll on baking sheet. Heat at 400°F (205°C) for 25 minutes. Open and roll foil back. Return to oven. Bake until thoroughly heated, browned and puffed, about 10 minutes. Cut into 1 to 1-1/4-inch slices. Garnish slices with pimiento.

# Sherried Pea Bisque

*Ladle this hearty main-dish soup out of an elegant tureen.*

1 cup UNCLE BEN'S® QUICK™
  Brand Rice
3/4 cup water
1/4 teaspoon salt
1/2 tablespoon butter or margarine
1 (11-1/2-oz.) can condensed
  tomato bisque soup

1 (11-1/2-oz.) can condensed
  split-pea-with-ham soup
2 soup-cans half and half
1/4 teaspoon basil
3 tablespoons dry sherry
1/4 cup chopped pecans

Prepare rice with water, salt and butter or margarine according to package directions for half the basic recipe; keep warm. Combine remaining ingredients except pecans. Heat thoroughly. Pour into bowls. Top each bowl of soup with rice and chopped pecans. Makes 4 to 6 servings.


# Clams Mornay

*Clams and creamy cheese sauce—a delectable duo.*

1 (8-oz.) can minced clams, drained;
  reserve liquid
1 (8-oz.) bottle clam juice
1/2 cup UNCLE BEN'S® CONVERTED®
  Brand Rice

2-1/2 tablespoons butter or margarine
2 tablespoons chopped shallots
  or green onions
1 tablespoon tomato paste
1 teaspoon dried chopped chives

*Cheese Sauce:*
2 tablespoons butter
2 tablespoons flour
1 cup milk

1/4 cup grated Parmesan cheese
1/4 cup shredded Swiss cheese

Add reserved liquid from clams to bottled clam juice to make 1-1/3 cups liquid. Cook rice with liquid and 1/2 tablespoon of the butter or margarine according to package direction for half the basic recipe, omitting the salt. In a small saucepan, melt remaining butter or margarine. Add shallots or green onions and sauté 5 minutes. Stir in tomato paste and chives. Add rice and clams. Mix well. Spoon into individual ramekins or small baking shells. Spoon Cheese Sauce over rice and clam mixture. Place in broiler, 3 inches below heat source, until lightly browned and bubbling. Serve hot. Makes 12 servings.

**Cheese Sauce:**
In a medium saucepan, melt 2 tablespoons butter. Blend in flour. Add milk and cook, stirring constantly, until thickened and smooth. Add cheeses and stir until cheese melts. Makes about 1-1/2 cup.

**Variation:**
Substitute white-sauce mix for cheese-sauce recipe and add cheeses.

# Stuffed Pepper Appetizers

*Your guests will want more of this unusual first course.*

2/3 cup finely chopped onions
2 cloves garlic, minced
2 tablespoons olive oil
3 cups chicken broth
1-1/2 cups UNCLE BEN'S® CONVERTED®
   Brand Rice

2 teaspoons seasoned salt
1/8 teaspoon powdered saffron
6 medium green peppers
Water
12 anchovy fillets
Paprika for garnish

In a large saucepan, cook onions and garlic in olive oil until browned. Add chicken broth and bring to boil. Stir in rice and seasoned salt. Cover tightly. Simmer 20 minutes. Stir in saffron. Remove from heat. Let stand, covered, until all liquid is absorbed, about 5 minutes. Cut stems out of green peppers, remove seeds. Cut thin slice off bottoms to level. Stuff rice mixture firmly into peppers. Put in heavy casserole or Dutch oven with cover. Add 1/2 inch of water. Cover. Bring to a simmer over medium heat. Cook 10 to 15 minutes or until peppers are soft, but still crisp. Chill. Cut in half lengthwise and garnish each half with an anchovy fillet and paprika. Serves 12.

# Crabmeat Salad Bites

*Exquisitely dainty and delicious.*

1 (6-oz.) pkg. UNCLE BEN'S®
   Long Grain & Wild Rice
2-1/2 cups water
1 cup mayonnaise
2 tablespoons lemon juice
1/4 teaspoon salt
Dash of cayenne pepper

2 (6-oz.) pkgs. frozen crabmeat,
   thawed and drained
1 cup finely chopped celery
2 green onions, thinly sliced
5 dozen pastry barquettes or tiny tarts,
   see Variations below

Cook contents of rice and seasoning packets with water according to package directions. Cover and chill well. Combine rice, mayonnaise, lemon juice, salt and cayenne pepper. Mix well. Flake crabmeat. Fold in crabmeat, celery and green onion. Serve in cooled, baked pastry barquettes or tiny tarts. Makes about 5 cups salad mixture or enough for about 5 dozen appetizers.

### Variations:

1 (11-oz.) package of pie-crust mix will make 2 to 3 dozen pastry barquettes or tiny tarts, depending upon size.

Substitute toast rounds for pastry barquettes.

# Apricot-Yogurt Bread

*Yogurt and apricot nectar blend in an unusual rice bread.*

1/4 cup UNCLE BEN'S® CONVERTED®
  Brand Rice
2/3 cup water
1/4 teaspoon salt
1 teaspoon butter or margarine
1 (1-lb. 1-oz.) pkg. quick nut-bread mix

1/3 cup chopped dried apricots
2 tablespoons flour
1 (8-oz.) carton apricot yogurt
1/3 cup apricot nectar or water
1 egg, slightly beaten

Preheat oven to 350°F (177°C). Butter and flour a 9" x 5" loaf pan. Cook rice with 2/3 cup water, 1/4 teaspoon salt and 1 teaspoon butter or margarine according to package directions. Cool. In a large bowl, combine quick nut-bread mix, apricots and flour; mix. Add cooked rice, yogurt, apricot nectar or water and egg. Stir just until dry ingredients are moistened. Spoon batter into prepared pan. Bake until done and lightly browned, about 1 hour. Let cool in pan 10 minutes. Turn out on wire rack and cool. Makes 1 loaf.

# California-Style Beef Stew

*Party fare for an informal get-together.*

4 slices bacon diced
1-1/2 lbs. boneless beef chuck cut
  into 1 to 1-1/2-in. chunks
1 cup sliced onion
1 tablespoon flour
1 (1-lb.) can tomatoes
1 (10-1/2-oz.) can condensed beef broth
1/2 teaspoon chili powder
1 (15-1/2-oz.) can garbanzo beans, drained

2 cups sliced zucchini (about 1/2 lb.)
1 cup water
1/2 teaspoon salt
3 cups UNCLE BEN'S® QUICK™
  Brand Rice
2-1/3 cups water
3/4 teaspoon salt
1-1/2 tablespoons butter or margarine

In a large skillet, fry bacon until crisp. Remove bacon bits. Add beef chunks to drippings. Brown on all sides. Add onion. Cook until tender. Stir in flour. Add tomatoes, beef broth, chili powder and bacon bits. Stir and cover. Cook slowly until meat is almost tender, about 1-3/4 hours. Add garbanzo beans, zucchini, water and salt. Cover. Cook until meat and zucchini are tender, about 15 minutes. Cook rice with 2-1/3 cups water, 3/4 teaspoon salt and butter or margarine according to package directions. Serve stew in bowls over hot cooked rice. Makes 6 servings.

# How To Make
# Zucchini Appetizers

Cut cooled zucchini in half lengthwise and again crosswise, scooping out centers to make shells. Hollowed zucchini will break easily unless the shell is at least 1/4-inch thick.

Cook sausage and add finely chopped zucchini and onions. Cook until zucchini is tender, then stir in cooked rice. Let mixture cool slightly before adding eggs.

Fill salted zucchini shells with rice mixture and arrange in shallow baking pans.

# Zucchini Appetizers

*Pungent stuffing turns zucchini into party fare.*

1 (6-oz.) pkg. UNCLE BEN'S®
   Long Grain & Wild Rice
2-1/2 cups water
1 tablespoon butter or margarine
18 small zucchini, about 5" long
2 cups boiling water

1 lb. hot Italian sausage
4 green onions, sliced
1/2 cup chopped pistachio nuts or
   walnuts, if desired
2 eggs, beaten
1 teaspoon salt

Cook contents of rice and seasoning packets with water and butter or margarine according to package directions. Wash zucchini and cook in boiling water 5 to 8 minutes. Drain and cool slightly. Cut zucchini in half lengthwise then crosswise. Scoop out centers of each piece, leaving a 1/4-inch-shell on each. Finely chop zucchini centers. Remove sausage from casing and break meat into small pieces. Cook over moderate heat until crumbly. Add chopped zucchini and onions. Cook until zucchini is tender. Stir in cooked rice and nuts, if desired. Cool mixture slightly. Stir in eggs. Sprinkle zucchini shells with salt. Fill with rice mixture. Arrange in shallow baking pans. Cover with aluminum foil and chill. Before serving, bake at 350°F (177°C) until hot, 20 to 25 minutes. Makes 6 dozen appetizers.

**Variation:**
If small zucchini are not available, slice 10 larger ones, about 7-inches long, 1-inch thick. Scoop out centers and stuff.


# Bombay Bruffins

*Company for brunch? Try this muffin adventure.*

3/4 cup UNCLE BEN'S® QUICK™
   Brand Rice
1 cup milk
2 cups flour
1/2 cup sugar
3 teaspoons baking powder
1 teaspoon curry powder

1/2 teaspoon salt
1/2 cup seedless raisins
1 (8-oz.) can crushed pineapple,
   not drained
2 eggs, slightly beaten
1/4 cup butter or margarine, melted
1/4 cup apricot preserves

Preheat oven to 400°F (204°C). Butter sixteen 2-1/2" x 1-1/4" muffin cups. Combine rice and milk in a large saucepan. Bring to a boil. Cover and simmer until all milk is absorbed, about 5 minutes. Cool. Sift together flour, sugar, baking powder, curry powder and salt. Add raisins, pineapple, eggs and melted butter or margarine. Stir just until dry ingredients are moistened. Spoon into buttered muffin cups, using about 1/4 cup batter for each. Bake until lightly browned, about 20 minutes. Warm apricot preserves and spoon over hot bruffins. Let bruffins cool in pans 3 to 4 minutes before serving. Makes 16 bruffins.

# Cream of Wild Rice Soup

*Serve this superb cream soup as an elegant first course.*

1 (6-oz.) pkg. UNCLE BEN'S®
  Long Grain & Wild Rice
2-1/2 cups water
1 tablespoon butter or margarine
1 tablespoon butter or margarine
3/4 cup chopped onion

3 (13-3/4-oz.) cans chicken broth
2 cups half and half
1-1/2 teaspoons seasoned salt
1 tablespoon flour
1 cup dry white wine

Cook contents of rice and seasoning packets with water and 1 tablespoon butter or margarine according to package directions. Melt 1 tablespoon butter or margarine in Dutch oven. Add onion. Cook until tender, not brown. Add cooked rice, chicken broth, half and half and salt. Combine flour and wine. Stir until free of lumps. Stir into soup and continue stirring until mixture is smooth. Simmer to blend flavors, about 20 minutes. Makes 10 servings.


# Curried Rice Balls

*Herbed and curried rice balls in a crumb crust.*

1/4 cup butter or margarine
1/2 cup UNCLE BEN'S® CONVERTED®
  Brand Rice
4 chicken-bouillon cubes, crushed
1-1/4 cups water
1/2 teaspoon salt
1/4 teaspoon oregano, crushed

3 eggs, beaten
1/2 cup fine corn-flake crumbs
1/2 teaspoon curry powder
Fine corn-flake crumbs for coating
Vegetable oil for deep-fat frying
  (1 to 2 cups)

*Chutney Dip:*
1 tablespoon flour
1/4 teaspoon salt
1/4 teaspoon sugar
1/4 teaspoon dry mustard
1/4 teaspoon curry powder

2 egg yolks, beaten
1 cup milk
1/4 cup finely chopped chutney
1 tablespoon lemon juice

In a large skillet, melt butter or margarine. Add rice and sauté until golden brown. Add bouillon cubes, water, salt and oregano. Mix well. Bring to a boil. Cover tightly and simmer 20 minutes. Remove from heat. Let stand, covered, until all water is absorbed, about 5 minutes. Combine eggs, corn-flake crumbs and 1/2 teaspoon curry powder. Add to rice; mix thoroughly. Shape mixture into 24 balls. Generously coat balls with corn-flake crumbs. Chill until ready to use. Deep-fat fry at 375°F (191°C) until coating is golden brown, and rice balls are hot, 2 to 3 minutes. Serve with Chutney Dip. Makes 6 servings.

**Chutney Dip:**
Mix together flour, salt, sugar, mustard and curry powder. Add egg yolks and milk. Mix well. Cook over very low heat, stirring constantly until thickened. Stir in chutney and lemon juice. Makes 1-1/4 to 1-1/2 cups.

# Pimiento-Cheese Party Ball

*Fantastic beginning to a memorable dinner.*

1 cup UNCLE BEN'S® QUICK™
   Brand Rice
3/4 cup water
1/4 teaspoon salt
1/2 tablespoon butter or margarine
3 (5-oz.) jars pimiento-cheese spread

1 cup chopped pimiento-stuffed olives
3 tablespoons grated onion
3 tablespoons grated green pepper
2 teaspoons prepared horseradish sauce
1/4 teaspoon Tabasco® sauce
1/2 cup finely chopped pecans

Cook rice according to package directions for half the basic recipe. Chill. Combine all ingredients, except pecans; mix well. Line a small bowl with plastic wrap. Spoon cheese mixture into bowl. Fold edges of plastic wrap over rice mixture. Remove from bowl and shape into a ball. Chill well, 5 to 6 hours or overnight. Remove plastic wrap from ball. Roll ball in chopped pecans until evenly coated with nuts. Serve with assorted crackers. Makes 12 to 16 servings.

### Variations:
Substitute bacon-cheese spread or jalapeño-cheese spread for pimiento-cheese spread if desired.

# Taco Soup

*Close the generation gap with this hearty "in" soup.*

1 lb. lean ground beef
1/4 cup chopped onion
1 small clove garlic, minced
1 (6-oz.) can tomato paste
1 tablespoon vinegar
1 (1-1/4-oz.) envelope taco-
   seasoning mix
1 teaspoon chili powder

3 cups water
1 cup UNCLE BEN'S® QUICK™
   Brand Rice
1 (8-oz.) can red kidney beans
3/4 cup shredded Monterey Jack or
   Cheddar cheese
Taco-flavored corn chips

In a 3-quart saucepan, brown meat, onion and garlic. Add tomato paste, vinegar, taco-seasoning mix and chili powder. Mix well. Stir in water. Bring to a boil. Simmer about 30 minutes. Add rice and undrained kidney beans. Cover. Simmer to cook rice and blend flavors, about 30 minutes. Ladle into soup bowls. Top each serving with shredded cheese. Serve with corn chips. Makes 6 servings.

# Salad Appetizers

*Cool crisp cucumber slices and bright cherry tomatoes hold salad tidbits.*

1 (6-oz.) pkg. UNCLE BEN'S®
  Long Grain & Wild Rice
2-1/2 cups water
1 tablespoon butter or margarine
1 cup finely diced cooked chicken or ham
1/2 cup finely chopped celery
2 tablespoons chopped green onion

1 tablespoon chopped parsley
1/3 cup mayonnaise or mayonnaise-type
  salad dressing
1 tablespoon lemon juice
4 doz. cherry tomatoes
4 doz. cucumber slices
Thin pimiento strips

Cook contents of rice and seasoning packets with water and butter or margarine according to package directions. Chill. Combine rice, chicken or ham, celery, green onion, parsley, salad dressing or mayonnaise and lemon juice. Mix well. Chill. To fill tomatoes, cut a thin slice from top of washed tomatoes; remove seeds with spoon and drain well. Stuff tomatoes with salad mixture. Slice cucumber about 3/8-inch thick and top each slice with a heaping teaspoonful of salad mixture. Garnish with pimiento. Makes 4 cups salad mixture. About 1 cup salad mixture will fill 2 dozen cherry tomatoes or top 2 dozen cucumber slices.

# Spectacular Appetizer

*Rich rice cakes elegantly topped with caviar and sour cream.*

2 cups UNCLE BEN'S® QUICK™
  Brand Rice
1-2/3 cups water
1/2 teaspoon salt
1 (1-1/2-oz.) pkg. white-sauce mix
1 to 2 cups milk
3 egg yolks, slightly beaten

1/2 cup whipping cream
1/4 teaspoon salt
Dash ground nutmeg
1 to 2 tablespoons butter
Dairy sour cream, for garnish
Caviar (black or red) or anchovy
  fillets, for garnish

Cook rice with water and salt according to package directions, omitting butter. Prepare a thick sauce with white-sauce mix and milk following directions on package. Add hot rice, egg yolks, whipping cream, salt and nutmeg to sauce. Mix well. Heat butter in a large skillet. Drop rice mixture by tablespoonfuls into hot skillet. Flatten slightly. Fry slowly until browned on both sides, turning once. Serve topped with sour cream and caviar or an anchovy fillet. Makes about 3 dozen.

**Variation:**
To cook rice cakes ahead of time, chill until ready to serve. Just before serving, arrange cakes on a buttered baking sheet. Bake at 400°F (205°C) until heated, 5 to 7 minutes. Top with sour cream and caviar.

# Salads

Rice salads are unusual, delicious and easy to make. Did you know they can be served hot or cold? There is such a variety in this section that you're sure to find more than one rice salad you'll like. Hot Chicken Salad is delicious. When the weather is too hot to cook, serve a meal in a salad with Nicoise Salad. Seasonal Fruit Salad and Brown Rice Garden Salad are appealing ways to get fresh vegetables into menus. UNCLE BEN'S® Rice salads are tasty and time-saving ways to serve vegetables and rice.

*Ladies Luncheon*
* Seasonal Fruit Salad
  Hot Rolls
  Mocha Nut Torte

*Let's Use the Grill*
  Barbecued Spareribs
* Barbecue Bonus Salad
  Corn
  Watermelon

*Too Hot To Cook*
* Niçoise Salad
  Warmed French Bread, Butter
  Apple Flan

*A Toast To Nutrition*
  Assorted Cheese Board
* Brown Rice Garden Salad
  Bran Muffins
  Sliced Peaches & Blueberries

*Family Favorite*
* Hot Chicken Salad
  Frenched Green Beans
  Red Cabbage Slaw
  Cherry Pie

*A Southwestern Flavor*
* Chili & Sour Cream Salad
  Sliced Tomatoes
  Buttered Hot Rye Bread
  Strawberry Crepes

*These recipes are in this section.*

# Gazpacho Salad

*Here's a chance to use your garden favorites.*

2 cups chilled, *cooked* UNCLE BEN'S®
  CONVERTED® Brand Rice
1/2 cup peeled, seeded and diced cucumbers
1/4 cup chopped parsley
1/4 cup green onion
1/4 cup diced green pepper
1 tomato, peeled, seeded and diced

1/3 cup olive oil
3 tablespoons lemon juice
2 cloves garlic, minced
1 teaspoon salt
1/2 teaspoon sugar
Dash pepper
Crisp salad greens

In a large bowl, combine cooked rice, cucumbers, parsley, onion, green pepper and tomato. Toss lightly. In a jar, combine remaining ingredients except salad greens. Cover and shake well. Pour over rice-vegetable mixture and toss lightly. Chill several hours. Serve on crisp salad greens. Makes 4 to 6 servings.

# Seafood Salad With Orange Vinaigrette

*Try this unbeatable tasty blend.*

1 cup UNCLE BEN'S® CONVERTED®
  Brand Rice
2-1/2 cups water
1 teaspoon salt
1 tablespoon butter or margarine
About 3/4 cup Orange Vinaigrette, see below
3/4 lb. fresh shrimp, cleaned, deveined,
  and cooked

1/2 lb. crabmeat
1/2 lb. cooked and chilled bay scallops,
  if desired
2 tablespoons chopped green chilies
2 green onions, thinly sliced
Crisp salad greens
Green pepper rings, for garnish

*Orange Vinaigrette:*
1/2 cup olive oil
2 tablespoons lemon juice
2 tablespoons grated orange peel

1 teaspoon salt
1/2 teaspoon freshly ground black pepper

Cook rice with water, salt and butter or margarine according to package directions. While hot, toss with Orange Vinaigrette in a large bowl. Cover and chill well. Add seafood, chilies and green onions; toss lightly. Serve on crisp salad greens. Garnish with green pepper rings. Makes 6 servings.

**Orange Vinaigrette:**
Combine ingredients in a jar. Cover and shake to mix well. Makes about 3/4 cup.

# Carmen Salad

*Brings a touch of Spain to your dining.*

1-1/2 cups UNCLE BEN'S® QUICK™
   Brand Rice
1-1/3 cups water
1/4 teaspoon salt
1/8 teaspoon saffron
1 cup diced ham

1 cup cooked and chilled fresh or frozen peas
1/2 cup sliced pimiento-stuffed olives
3 tablespoons olive oil
3 tablespoons vinegar
2 medium tomatoes, sliced
3 hard-cooked eggs, sliced

Stir rice, water, salt and saffron into a large saucepan. Bring to a *vigorous* boil. Reduce heat. Cover and simmer until liquid is absorbed, about 5 minutes. Chill. In a large mixing bowl, combine rice, ham, peas and olives. Add olive oil and vinegar. Mix carefully until all ingredients are evenly coated with oil and vinegar. Chill about 1 hour. Spoon salad in center of large salad plate. Cut tomato slices in half. Arrange tomato and egg slices around salad. Makes 6 servings.

# Chili & Sour Cream Salad

*Very Mexican—very rich!*

1 (7-oz.) pkg. frozen diced cooked chicken,
   (about 1-1/2 cups)
1-1/2 cups *cooked* and chilled UNCLE BEN'S®
   CONVERTED® Brand Rice
1 (3-1/2-oz.) can pitted ripe olives,
   drained and sliced
1 cup dairy sour cream (1/2-pt.)

1/2 cup shredded Monterey Jack cheese
1/4 cup mayonnaise
3 tablespoons chopped roasted and
   peeled green chilies
2 or 3 tablespoons sliced green onion
1 (7-oz.) can tuna, drained and flaked
4 to 6 medium tomatoes

Thaw chicken. In a large bowl, combine cooked rice, olives, sour cream, cheese, mayonnaise, green chilies and green onion. Mix well. Carefully stir in chicken and tuna. Chill at least 1 hour before serving. Cut tomatoes in wedges almost through. Do not cut through bottom of tomato. Fill tomato centers with rice salad. Makes 4 to 6 servings.

**Variations:**

Substitute 3/4 teaspoon chili powder for green chilies, or to taste.

Substitute 1 or 2 (4-1/2-oz.) cans shrimp, drained and rinsed for tuna.

# Brown Rice Garden Salad

*Crisp vegetables in chewy brown rice.*

1 cup UNCLE BEN'S® Brown Rice
2-2/3 cups water
1 teaspoon salt
1 tablespoon butter or margarine
1 cup mayonnaise or mayonnaise-style
  salad dressing

4 green onions, sliced
1/2 teaspoon salt
2 medium zucchini, sliced
1 medium tomato, chopped and drained
1 teaspoon dill weed

Cook rice with water, salt and butter or margarine according to package directions. Place cooked rice in a large bowl. Cover and refrigerate. Add salad dressing and onions. Mix well. Chill 1 hour. Stir in remaining ingredients. Chill before serving. Makes 6 servings.

# Seasonal Fruit Salad

*A sensational combination of fruits, nuts and seasonings.*

1 cup UNCLE BEN'S® CONVERTED®
  Brand Rice
2-1/2 cups water
1 teaspoon salt
1 tablespoon butter or margarine
2 tablespoons vegetable oil (not olive oil)
2 medium navel oranges, peeled
  and sectioned

1 (8-oz.) can pineapple chunks,
  chilled and drained
1 cup melon balls
1/2 cup sliced strawberries
1/2 cup coarsely chopped pecans
About 1 cup Poppy Seed Dressing, see below
Crisp salad greens
Whole strawberries and pecans for garnish

*Poppy Seed Dressing:*
1/3 cup sugar
3 tablespoons vinegar
2 teaspoons onion juice
1/2 teaspoon dry mustard

1/2 teaspoon salt
1/2 cup vegetable oil (not olive oil)
2 teaspoons poppy seeds

Cook rice with water, salt and butter or margarine according to package directions. While hot, toss with oil in a large bowl. Cover and chill well. Add pineapple, melon, strawberries, chopped pecans and Poppy Seed Dressing. Toss lightly. Serve on crisp salad greens. Garnish with strawberries and pecans. Makes 6 servings.

**Poppy Seed Dressing:**
Combine sugar, vinegar, onion juice, mustard and salt. Beat for about 3 minutes with electric mixer or blender. Gradually beat in oil, a little at a time. Beat until thick. When thick, beat in poppy seeds until well blended. Refrigerate, covered, until ready to use. Makes about 1 cup.

# How to Make Seasonal Fruit Salad

Reserve poppy seeds. Beat remaining ingredients for dressing until thick. Stir in poppy seeds.

Combine fruit, pecans and Poppy Seed Dressing with chilled, cooked rice.

Serve on crisp salad greens. Garnish with strawberries and pecans.

# Fresh Vegetable Salad

*A refreshing garden-to-table dish.*

2 cups chilled, *cooked* UNCLE BEN'S®
  CONVERTED® Brand Rice
2 large onions, finely chopped
3 stalks celery, thinly sliced and tops
  finely chopped
1 large carrot, peeled and shredded
4 hard-cooked eggs, sliced
1/2 cup halved seedless green grapes
1/2 cup slivered almonds

1/2 cup sliced fresh mushrooms
1/2 cup sliced fresh mushrooms
1 cup mayonnaise or mayonnaise-style
  salad dressing
1 tablespoon mustard
1/2 teaspoon seasoned salt
1/8 teaspoon Worcestershire sauce
1/8 teaspoon seasoned pepper
Watercress, if desired

In a large bowl combine rice, onions, celery, carrot, eggs, grapes, almonds and mushrooms. Toss to mix. Combine mayonnaise or salad dressing, mustard, celery seed, seasoned salt, Worcestershire sauce and seasoned pepper. Mix well. Fold into rice mixture. Chill 2 to 3 hours. Serve in individual salad bowls. Garnish outer edge of bowls with sprigs of watercress, if desired. Makes 6 servings.

# Spinach Salad With Oriental Vinaigrette

*Nuts give crunch to this spicy salad.*

1 cup UNCLE BEN'S® CONVERTED®
  Brand Rice
2-1/2 cups water
1 teaspoon salt
1 tablespoon butter or margarine
2/3 cup Garlic-Soy-Sauce Vinaigrette, see below

1/4 lb. fresh spinach leaves, cut in julienne strips
4 green onions, finely chopped
1 small zucchini, cut in julienne strips
1/2 cup julienne celery strips
3/4 cup pine nuts or chopped walnuts
Crisp salad greens

*Garlic-Soy-Sauce Vinaigrette:*
1/2 cup olive oil
1 tablespoon vinegar
1 tablespoon soy sauce

1/2 teaspoon freshly ground black pepper
2 cloves garlic, finely chopped

Cook rice with water, salt and butter or margarine according to package directions. While hot, toss with Garlic-Soy-Sauce Vinaigrette in a large bowl. Cover and chill well. Add spinach, onions, zucchini, celery and nuts. Toss lightly. Serve on crisp salad greens. Makes 6 to 8 servings.

**Garlic-Soy-Sauce Vinaigrette:**
Combine ingredients in a jar. Cover and shake to mix well. Makes about 2/3 cup.

# Hot Chicken Salad

*A meal in a jiffy from fast-cooking ingredients.*

2 tablespoons butter or margarine
2 whole large chicken breasts, skinned,
   boned and cut in strips
3 cups UNCLE BEN'S® QUICK™
   Brand Rice
2-1/3 cups water

2-1/2 teaspoons salt
1 cup sliced celery
1 medium tomato, diced
1/2 small green pepper, diced
1/2 cup mayonnaise-style salad dressing
   (but not mayonnaise)

In a large skillet, melt butter or margarine. Add chicken, cooking and stirring over moderately high heat until meat turns white. Add rice, water and salt. Stir. Bring to a *vigorous* boil. Reduce heat. Cover and simmer until liquid is absorbed, about 5 minutes. Stir in celery, tomato, green pepper and salad dressing. Heat through. Makes 4 to 6 servings.

# Niçoise Rice Salad

*Serve with a crusty loaf for an elegant cold supper.*

1 cup UNCLE BEN'S® CONVERTED®
   Brand Rice
2-1/2 cups water
1 teaspoon salt
1 tablespoon butter or margarine
About 2/3 cup Garlic-Basil Vinaigrette,
   see below
1 (6-1/2 or 7-oz.) can tuna, drained
   and flaked

1/2 cup coarsely chopped pitted black olives
1/2 cup julienne celery strips
6 green onions, cut in 1-inch lengths
1/2 small green pepper, chopped
1 cup cooked and chilled cut green beans
6 anchovies, chopped
Crisp salad greens
2 hard-cooked eggs, chopped, for garnish
Tomato wedges

*Garlic-Basil Vinaigrette:*
1/2 cup olive oil
2 tablespoons vinegar
1 teaspoon basil

1 teaspoon salt
1/2 teaspoon freshly ground black pepper
2 cloves garlic, finely chopped

Cook rice with water, salt and butter or margarine according to package directions. While hot, toss with Garlic-Basil Vinaigrette in a large bowl. Cover and chill well. Add tuna, olives, celery, onions, green pepper, green beans and anchovies. Toss lightly. Serve on crisp salad greens. Garnish with chopped eggs and tomato wedges. Makes 6 servings.

**Garlic-Basil Vinaigrette:**
Combine ingredients in a jar. Cover and shake to mix well. Makes about 2/3 cup.

**Variation:**
Arrange tuna, olives and vegetables on a lettuce-lined platter or plates around rice-salad mixture. Garnish with anchovy fillets.

# Hearty Peach Salad

*This salad will be in demand again and again.*

2 cups UNCLE BEN'S® QUICK™
  Brand Rice
1-2/3 cups water
1/2 teaspoon salt
1 tablespoon butter or margarine
2 tablespoons vegetable oil
2 tablespoons lemon juice
2 tablespoons honey

1/2 cup dairy sour cream
1 (1-lb.) can sliced cling peaches, well
  drained
1/2 lb. fully cooked ham, cut in julienne
  strips
1 cup sliced celery
1/2 cup chopped toasted almonds
Crisp salad greens

Cook rice with water, salt and butter or margarine according to package directions. Place in a large bowl. Cover and chill. Add oil, lemon juice and honey. Mix well. Chill 1 hour. Add sour cream and mix well. Add sliced peaches, ham, celery and almonds. Mix carefully. Chill at least 1 hour. Serve on crisp salad greens. Makes 5 to 6 servings.

# Fruited Salad

*Enjoy the Oriental flavor of seasoned rice and fresh fruit.*

1 (6-oz.) pkg. UNCLE BEN'S®
  Long Grain & Wild Rice
2-1/2 cups water
1 tablespoon butter or margarine
2 medium oranges
1 cup mayonnaise or mayonnaise-style
  salad dressing
1 cup sliced celery

1/2 cup chopped pecans
1/3 cup orange juice
1 teaspoon sugar
1/2 lb. seedless green grapes, washed
  and halved
6 cantaloupe or honeydew melon rings
Crisp salad greens

Cook contents of rice and seasoning packets with water and butter or margarine according to package directions. Chill. Wash oranges and grate 2 teaspoons of the orange peel; reserve. Peel oranges and remove white membrane. Dice oranges and set aside. Mix together rice, mayonnaise or salad dressing, celery, pecans, orange juice, orange peel and sugar. Chill well. Just before serving, add diced oranges and grapes. Mix well. To serve, arrange melon rings on crisp salad greens. Spoon salad onto melon rings. Makes 6 servings.

**Fruited Salad**

# Specialty of the House

*An unusual taste-tempting salad.*

1 cup UNCLE BEN'S® CONVERTED®
  Brand Rice
2-1/2 cups water
1 teaspoon salt
1 tablespoon butter or margarine
2 cups dairy sour cream or plain
  yogurt (1 pt.)

2 cups sliced celery
4 green onions, sliced
1/4 cup chopped parsley
1/2 teaspoon salt
2 cucumbers, pared and diced
1 tomato, diced
Dill weed to taste

Cook rice with water, 1 teaspoon salt and butter or margarine. Chill. In a large bowl, combine rice, sour cream or yogurt, celery, onions, parsley and 1/2 teaspoon salt. Mix. Chill well. Just before serving, stir in cucumbers, tomato and dill weed. Makes 6 to 8 servings.

Variations:
Add cucumbers or tomatoes in varying amounts to suit your taste.

# Lovin' Rice Salad

*Compliments galore go with this highly seasoned, colorful dish.*

2-1/2 cups water
2-1/2 cups water
1 chicken-bouillon cube, crushed
1/2 teaspoon coarse cracked pepper
1/4 teaspoon thyme
1/4 teaspoon turmeric
Pinch of ground cumin
1 cup UNCLE BEN'S® CONVERTED®
  Brand Rice

1/4 cup Italian salad dressing
1 cup finely diced celery
1 (4-oz.) jar pimiento, drained and sliced
1/2 cup pitted ripe olives, quartered
2 tablespoons minced chives
1 avocado, diced
Crisp salad greens
2 tomatoes, each cut in 6 wedges

In a 1-1/2-quart saucepan combine water, bouillon cube, onion salt, cracked pepper, thyme, turmeric and cumin. Bring to a boil. Stir in rice. Cover and simmer 20 minutes. Remove from heat. Let stand about 5 minutes. Cool. Add Italian salad dressing, celery, pimiento, ripe olives and chives. Toss lightly. Chill. Just before serving fold in avocado. Serve on crisp salad greens on individual salad plates. Garnish with tomato wedges. Makes 6 servings.

# Sweet & Sour Tuna Salad

*Tuna salad goes glamorous!*

1/2 cup UNCLE BEN'S® CONVERTED®
Brand Rice
2-1/2 cups water
1 teaspoon salt
1 tablespoon butter or margarine
1 (13-1/2-oz.) can pineapple tidbits or chunks
1/2 cup mayonnaise or mayonnaise-style
salad dressing

2 teaspoons soy sauce
1/2 teaspoon garlic salt
1 (6-1/2 or 7-oz.) can tuna, drained
and flaked
1 small green pepper, chopped
12 cherry tomatoes, cut in half
Crisp salad greens

Cook rice with water, salt and butter or margarine according to package directions. Chill well. Drain pineapple tidbits or chunks; reserve 2 tablespoons syrup. In a large bowl, combine mayonnaise or salad dressing, pineapple syrup, soy sauce and garlic salt. Mix well. Combine with chilled rice, pineapple tidbits or chunks, tuna and green pepper. Mix lightly. Chill until ready to serve. Fold in cherry-tomato halves. Serve on crisp salad greens. Makes 4 to 6 servings.

# Banana-Curried Salad

*Fruit, nuts and spices—an exotic, crunchy salad.*

1-1/2 cups UNCLE BEN'S® CONVERTED®
Brand Rice
3-1/3 cups water
1-1/2 teaspoons salt
1-1/2 tablespoons butter or margarine
4 medium bananas
1 tablespoon lemon juice
1/2 cup diagonally sliced celery
1/2 cup seedless raisins
1/2 cup chopped salted peanuts
2 tablespoons chopped pimiento

1 tablespoon minced chives
3/4 cup mayonnaise or mayonnaise-style
salad dressing
3 tablespoons cream
1 tablespoon lemon juice
1 tablespoon curry powder
1/2 teaspoon dry mustard
1/4 teaspoon hot-pepper sauce
Crisp salad greens
1/4 cup toasted flaked coconut,
if desired

Cook rice with water, salt and butter or margarine according to package directions. Chill. Cut bananas into 1/2-inch slices. Sprinkle 1 tablespoon lemon juice over banana slices. In a large bowl, combine rice, celery, raisins, peanuts, pimiento and chives. Toss lightly and chill. Combine mayonnaise or salad dressing, cream, 1 tablespoon lemon juice, curry powder, dry mustard and hot-pepper sauce. Mix well. Add to salad and toss lightly. Arrange salad on crisp salad greens on individual salad plates. Sprinkle with toasted coconut, if desired. Makes 8 servings.

# How To Make Salad Roll-Ups

Add onion, capers and fine herbs to rice. Moisten with Lemon Mayonnaise.

Spread a thin layer of rice on slices of ham or salmon. Don't make the rice layer too thick or rice will spill out as you roll up the slices.

Roll up each ham or salmon slice. Place on a tray with the cut sides down. Refrigerate until ready to serve.

# Meal-in-One Salad

*This nutritious dish is also a cool, refreshing meal.*

2 cups UNCLE BEN'S® QUICK™
   Brand Rice
1-2/3 cups water
1/2 teaspoon salt
1 tablespoon butter or margarine
1/2 lb. fresh spinach, torn into bite-
   size pieces
3/4 cup thinly sliced green onions and tops

1/4 lb. Swiss cheese cut in thin strips
1/2 cup thinly sliced radishes
1 teaspoon salt
1 teaspoon seasoned pepper
1/3 cup oil and vinegar dressing
Crisp salad greens
4 hard-cooked eggs, chopped
6 slices bacon, cooked crisp and crumbled

Cook rice with water, 1/2 teaspoon salt and butter or margarine according to package directions. Chill. Combine rice, spinach, onions, Swiss cheese, radishes, 1 teaspoon salt and seasoned pepper. Toss lightly. Cover and chill. Just before serving add oil and vinegar dressing and toss lightly. Spoon onto crisp salad greens in individual salad bowls. Sprinkle with eggs and bacon. Makes 6 servings.

# Salad Roll-ups

*Roll tasty herbed rice in salmon or ham slices.*

2 cups UNCLE BEN'S® QUICK™
   Brand Rice
1-2/3 cups water
1/2 teaspoon salt
1 tablespoon butter or margarine
1/4 cup chopped onion

2 tablespoons chopped capers
1/2 teaspoon dried fine herbs
About 6 to 8 tablespoons Lemon
   Mayonnaise, see below
12 thin slices (about 2-in. x 4-in.) smoked
   salmon or boiled ham, halved

*Lemon Mayonnaise:*
1/2 cup mayonnaise
2 teaspoons lemon juice

Cook rice with water, salt and butter or margarine according to package directions. Put in a medium bowl and add onion, capers and fine herbs. Add Lemon Mayonnaise to moisten. Spread on salmon or ham slices. Roll and arrange on tray, cut sides down. Chill until ready to serve. Makes 24 rolls.

Lemon Mayonnaise:
Combine ingredients in a small bowl. Refrigerate until ready to use. Makes 1 cup.

**Variation:**
Substitute 1/4 teaspoon each: dried parsley, thyme and marjoram for fine herbs.

# Barbecue Bonus Salad

*Mellow cheese slices and crisp crackers go well with this tangy salad.*

1 cup UNCLE BEN'S® CONVERTED®
  Brand Rice
2-1/2 cups water
1 teaspoon salt
1 tablespoon butter or margarine
2 cups mayonnaise or mayonnaise-style
  salad dressing
1 medium onion, finely chopped
2 cups sliced celery

4 teaspoons mustard
1/2 teaspoon salt
3 tablespoons crisp-cooked bacon bits
1 hard-cooked egg, chopped
Sliced radishes to taste
1 cucumber, pared and diced
Crisp salad greens
Tomato wedges for garnish

Cook rice with water, 1 teaspoon salt and butter or margarine according to package directions. Chill. Combine rice, mayonnaise or salad dressing, onion, celery, mustard and 1/2 teaspoon salt. Mix. Chill well. Just before serving, stir in bacon bits, egg, radishes and cucumber. Serve in bowl lined with crisp salad greens. Garnish with tomato wedges. Makes 6 to 8 servings.

# Polynesian Ham Salad

*Sprinkle with toasted almonds for a gourmet touch.*

3 cups UNCLE BEN'S® QUICK™
  Brand Rice
2-1/3 cups water
3/4 teaspoon salt
1-1/2 tablespoons butter or margarine
2 cups diagonally sliced celery
2 cups cubed (1/2-in. to 3/4-in.) cooked ham
2 (11-oz.) cans mandarin orange segments,
  drained
1/2 medium green pepper, cut in thin
  1-inch-long strips

1/2 cup dairy sour cream
1/4 cup mayonnaise or mayonnaise-style
  salad dressing
2 teaspoons lemon juice
1 teaspoon salt
1 teaspoon seasoned pepper
1 teaspoon onion powder
Crisp salad greens
1/4 cup toasted sliced almonds

Cook rice with water, 3/4 teaspoon salt and butter or margarine according to package directions. Chill. In a large bowl, combine rice, celery, ham, orange segments and green pepper. Combine sour cream, mayonnaise or salad dressing, lemon juice, 1 teaspoon salt, seasoned pepper and onion powder. Fold into rice mixture. Chill well. Serve on crisp salad greens. Sprinkle with almonds. Makes 6 servings.

# Imperial Salad

*Fit for an emperor's table!*

4 cups UNCLE BEN'S® QUICK™
   Brand Rice
3 cups water
1 teaspoon salt
1/2 tablespoon butter or margarine
3 tomatoes, cut in thin strips
1 green pepper, cut in strips
1 clove garlic, mashed

4 green onions, very finely sliced
1 (8-oz.) can peas
1 (4-oz.) can black olives, chopped
1/4 cup slivered pimiento
3 tablespoons wine vinegar
1 teaspoon dry mustard
Salt and pepper to taste
Watercress, for garnish

Cook rice with water, 1 teaspoon salt and butter or margarine according to package directions. In a large bowl combine all remaining ingredients. Toss with rice to mix. Chill before serving. To serve, mound on a platter. Garnish with watercress. Makes 6 to 8 servings.

**Variations:**
Garnish with tomato strips, black olives or cucumber slices.

# Chicken Salad With Tarragon Vinaigrette

*A refreshing salad—and it's hearty, too.*

1 cup UNCLE BEN'S® CONVERTED®
   Brand Rice
2-1/2 cups water
1 teaspoon salt
1 tablespoon butter or margarine
2/3 cup Tarragon Vinaigrette, see below

2-1/2 cups cooked julienne turkey or
   chicken strips (about 1/2 lb.)
1 cup diced celery
3/4 cup toasted slivered almonds
1/4 cup chopped parsley
Crisp salad greens
Tomato wedges

*Tarragon Vinaigrette:*
1/2 cup olive oil
2 tablespoons lemon juice
1 teaspoon tarragon

1 teaspoon salt
1/2 teaspoon freshly ground black pepper

Cook rice with water, salt and butter or margarine according to package directions. While hot, toss with Tarragon Vinaigrette in a large bowl. Cover and chill well. Add turkey or chicken, celery, almonds and parsley. Toss lightly. Serve on crisp salad greens. Garnish with tomato wedges. Makes 6 to 8 servings.

**Tarragon Vinaigrette:**
Combine ingredients in a jar. Cover and shake to mix well. Makes about 2/3 cup.

# Vegetables

UNCLE BEN'S® knows the value of fresh garden vegetables. And here are the recipes to prove it. Everyone will love these delicious rice-vegetable dishes. Even non-vegetarians cook Mixed Vegetable Curry again and again. Two-dish meals—one of meat or fish and a rice with vegetable treat—make easy cooking and cleaning up. Try exotic South Seas Rice & Snow Peas or elegant Stuffed Artichokes. You can increase the nutritional value of rice by cooking it in vegetable or meat stock. The rice will absorb both the stock flavors and nutritive values.

### The Flavors of Greece
 Braised Shoulder Lamb Chops
\* Spinach and Brown Rice Greek-Style
 Sliced Tomato-Lettuce Salad
 Sour Cream Dressing
 Ice Cream
 Honey Nut Topping

### Summer's Bounty
 Broiled Chicken
\* Ratatouille Rice Cups
 Fresh Spinach Salad
 Lemon Dressing
 Strawberries

### Thanksgiving Dinner
 Roast Turkey
 Stuffing
\* Wild Rice Ring with Creamed Onions
 Pureed Broccoli in Tomato cups
 Assorted Relishes
 Hot Rolls
 Pumpkin Pie

### Patio Party
 Grilled Steak
\* Stuffed Artichokes
 Mixed Green Salad
 Italian Dressing
 Chocolate Eclairs

### Who Misses Meat?
\* Mixed Vegetable Curry
 Sliced Cucumbers in Sour Cream with Chives
 Baked Bananas and Coconut in Orange Sauce

### Polynesian Supper
 Stir-Fried Shrimp Almond
\* South Seas Rice and Snow Peas
 Lime Dressed Papaya, Pineapple and
 Coconut Salad
 Orange Sherbet

*These recipes are in this section.*

# Spanish Rice

*The more crushed red peppers you use—the "zippier" the rice!*

2 tablespoons bacon drippings
1 cup UNCLE BEN'S® CONVERTED®
   Brand Rice
1 onion, chopped
1/2 green pepper, chopped
1 stalk celery, diced
1 (6-oz.) can tomato paste

1 (8-oz.) can tomato sauce
1 bay leaf, crushed
2 cloves garlic, minced
1/2 teaspoon crushed red peppers, to taste
1/2 teaspoon thyme
2-3/4 cups water
Salt and pepper to taste

In a large skillet, heat drippings. Add uncooked rice. Cook over moderate heat, stirring constantly, until rice is lightly browned. Add onion, green pepper and celery. Cook until tender. Stir in remaining ingredients. Bring to a boil. Reduce heat and cover. Simmer 20 minutes. Remove from heat. Let stand, covered, until most of liquid is absorbed, about 5 minutes. Makes 6 servings.

# Mixed-Vegetable Curry

*An amazingly satisfying meatless dish.*

1 teaspoon salt
1 clove garlic
2 tablespoons butter or margarine
1 lb. carrots, cleaned and sliced diagonally
1 medium onion, sliced
1-1/2 teaspoons coriander
1 teaspoon turmeric
1/2 teaspoon ground ginger

1/8 teaspoon cayenne pepper
1/2 cup water
1 small head cauliflower (about 1 lb.), broken
   into flowerets
1/2 cup water
2 teaspoons cornstarch
Spiced Rice, see below

*Spiced Rice:*
1 cup UNCLE BEN'S® CONVERTED®
   Brand Rice
2-1/2 cups water
1 teaspoon salt
1 tablespoon butter

1/3 cup chopped walnuts
1/3 cup seedless raisins
1/4 teaspoon cinnamon
1/8 teaspoon ground cloves

Mash salt and garlic together. Melt butter or margarine in a large saucepan. Add carrots, onion and salt-garlic mixture. Stir and heat through. Add coriander, turmeric, ginger and cayenne pepper; stir. Add 1/2 cup water and cover. Cook over low heat about 10 minutes. Add cauliflower and stir. Cover. Cook until vegetables are tender, about 10 minutes longer. Combine 1/2 cup water and cornstarch. Stir until free of lumps. Add to vegetables. Heat and stir until liquid is thickened. Serve with Spiced Rice. Makes 4 main-meal servings or 6 side-dish servings.

Spiced Rice:
Cook rice with water, salt and butter or margarine according to package directions. Stir walnuts, raisins, cinnamon and cloves into hot cooked rice.

# Onion Brown Rice With Carrots

*Try this in your crockery cooker—it's superb!*

2-2/3 cups water
1 cup UNCLE BEN'S® Brown Rice
1 tablespoon butter or margarine
1-1/2 teaspoons salt
1/2 lb. carrots, sliced

1 medium onion, sliced
1/2 cup chopped salted cashews
1/3 cup orange-juice concentrate, thawed
4 green onions, sliced

In a large saucepan, bring water to a boil. Add rice, butter or margarine, salt, carrots and sliced onion. Stir and cover tightly. Cook over low heat until all liquid is absorbed, about 50 minutes. Stir in cashews, orange-juice concentrate and green onions. Makes 6 servings.

**To Make in a Crockery Cooker:**
Rub butter or margarine over bottom and up sides of crockery cooker. Put in carrots, onion and rice. Sprinkle with salt. Add water and cover. Cook on High until all liquid is absorbed, about 3 hours. Stir in cashews, orange-juice concentrate and green onions.

# Cheese-Spinach Casserole

*A yummy way to serve Popeye's favorite.*

1 (6-oz.) pkg. UNCLE BEN'S®
  Long Grain & Wild Rice
1 (4-oz.) can sliced mushrooms, drained
2 teaspoons prepared mustard
1/2 teaspoon salt

2-1/4 cups water
1 (10-oz.) pkg. frozen chopped or leaf spinach
3/4 cup chopped onion
1 tablespoon butter or margarine
1 (8-oz.) pkg. cream cheese, cubed

Preheat oven to 375°F (191°C). Place contents of rice and seasoning packets, mushrooms, mustard and salt in 2-quart casserole. In a large saucepan, combine water, spinach, onion and butter or margarine. Bring to a boil. Pour over rice mixture and stir. Cover tightly and bake 30 minutes. Uncover. Stir in cream cheese. Bake, uncovered, 10 to 15 minutes. Makes 6 to 8 servings.

**Variation:**
For a buffet dish, place the rice mixture and cream cheese in a ring mold before the final baking. Unmold when done and fill center with pearl onions in a cream sauce.

# Ratatouille Rice Cups

*Garden vegetables dress up for company.*

1-1/2 cups sliced onion
1 clove garlic, minced
1/4 cup olive oil
1 cup UNCLE BEN'S® Brown Rice
2-1/3 cups water
2-1/2 teaspoons salt

1-1/2 teaspoons basil
4 medium (3-1/2-in.-diameter) tomatoes
1 green or red pepper, chopped
1 small eggplant, diced
1 medium zucchini, thinly sliced
Chopped parsley for garnish

In a large skillet, cook onion and garlic in olive oil until onion is tender, not brown. Stir in rice, water, salt and basil. Bring to a boil. Reduce heat and cover. Simmer until liquid is absorbed, about 50 minutes. Halve and hollow tomatoes to form shells 1/4-inch thick. Chop pulp and drain. Stir chopped tomato pulp into rice with green or red pepper, eggplant and zucchini. Cook, covered, until vegetables are heated and tender, about 10 minutes. Uncover to evaporate any extra liquid. Fill tomato shells with mixture. Sprinkle with parsley before serving. Makes 8 servings.

# Florentine Rice Ring

*A taste of romantic Italy for your buffet luncheon.*

2 (10-oz.) pkgs. frozen chopped spinach
Salted water
4 cups UNCLE BEN'S® QUICK™
  Brand Rice
3 cups water
1 teaspoon salt

1/4 teaspoon garlic salt
2 tablespoons butter or margarine
1-1/2 cups grated or shredded
  Parmesan cheese
2 tablespoons butter or margarine

Oil a 6-cup ring mold. Cook spinach in salted water as directed on package; drain well. Stir rice, water, salt, garlic salt and 2 tablespoons butter or margarine into saucepan. Bring to *vigorous* boil. Cover and simmer about 5 minutes. Measure and reserve 2 tablespoons Parmesan cheese to garnish ring. Combine cooked rice, spinach, 2 tablespoons butter or margarine and Parmesan cheese. Mix lightly. Spoon into oiled ring mold; press lightly. Unmold ring onto heated serving plate. Sprinkle reserved Parmesan cheese on top of ring. Makes 8 servings.

# Green-Rice Soufflé

*A mouth-watering soufflé adds glamour to a brunch or dinner party.*

1 cup grated Parmesan cheese
1 cup UNCLE BEN'S® CONVERTED®
  Brand Rice
2-1/2 cups water
1 teaspoon salt
1 tablespoon butter or margarine
1 medium onion, chopped
1 small green pepper, chopped

1/4 cup butter or margarine
1 (10-oz.) pkg. frozen chopped spinach,
  thawed and drained
1/4 cup flour
1 teaspoon salt
1 cup milk
4 eggs, separated

Preheat oven to 375°F (191°C). Butter a 2-quart soufflé dish or deep, round baking dish. Sprinkle bottom and sides evenly with about 2 tablespoons Parmesan cheese. Cook rice with water, 1 teaspoon salt and 1 tablespoon butter or margarine according to package directions. Cook onion and green pepper in 1/4 cup butter or margarine until onion is tender, not brown. Add chopped spinach. Cook until tender, about 5 minutes. Stir in flour and salt. Add milk. Cook until sauce is thickened, stirring constantly. Remove from heat. Stir in remaining Parmesan cheese and cooked rice. In a large bowl, beat egg yolks until thick and lemon-colored. Add rice mixture slowly, stirring constantly. Beat egg whites until stiff, but not dry. Fold into rice mixture. Pour into buttered baking dish. Bake until puffed and browned and knife inserted in center comes out clean, 35 to 40 minutes. Makes 6 servings.

# Broccoli-Cheese Casserole

*Easy, elegant and overflowing with mushrooms.*

1 (6-oz.) pkg. UNCLE BEN'S®
  Long Grain & Wild Rice
2-1/2 cups water
1 tablespoon butter or margarine
2 (10-oz.) pkgs. frozen broccoli
  spears

2 tablespoons butter or margarine
20 medium-size fresh mushrooms,
  washed and sliced
1 cup chopped red onion
1 lb. Monterey Jack cheese,
  coarsely shredded

Preheat oven to 375°F (191°C). Lightly butter a 13-1/2" x 8-1/2" baking dish. Cook contents of rice and seasoning packets with water and 1 tablespoon butter or margarine according to package directions. Keep warm. Cook broccoli spears according to package directions. Do not overcook. Drain and keep warm. In a large skillet, melt butter or margarine. Add mushrooms and onion. Cook until mushrooms are tender, stirring often, about 10 minutes. Stir in cooked rice. Arrange 1/2 the rice mixture, broccoli spears and cheese in layers in buttered baking dish. Repeat process, ending with cheese. Cover with aluminum foil, crimping it tightly to edges of dish. Bake until hot and bubbly and cheese is melted, about 15 minutes. Makes 6 to 8 servings.

# Bacon-Vegetable Platter

*Onion-flavored rice in a gala vegetable circle.*

1/4 cup sliced green onion
2 tablespoons butter or margarine
1 cup UNCLE BEN'S® Brown Rice
2-2/3 cups water
1 teaspoon salt

2 tablespoons chopped parsley
6 slices bacon, fried crisp and rolled into curls
Baked Tomatoes, see below
Herbed Zucchini Strips, see below
Steamed Corn, see below

*Baked Tomatoes:*
3 tomatoes
1/4 teaspoon salt
2 tablespoons fine dry bread crumbs

2 tablespoons grated Parmesan cheese
2 tablespoons olive oil
1/2 teaspoon basil

*Herbed Zucchini:*
6 small zucchini
2 tablespoons butter or margarine
2 tablespoons water

1/2 teaspoon basil
1/4 teaspoon salt

*Steamed Corn:*
6 ears corn
About 1 cup boiling salted water

In a large saucepan, cook onion in butter or margarine until tender, not brown. Add brown rice, water and salt. Bring to a boil and cover tightly. Cook over low heat until all water is absorbed, about 50 minutes. Stir in parsley. Keep rice warm while preparing vegetables. Before serving, mound rice mixture in center of serving platter. Circle with bacon curls, Baked Tomatoes, Herbed Zucchini Strips and Steamed Corn. Makes 6 servings.

**Baked Tomatoes:**
Preheat oven to 375°F (191°C). Cut tomatoes in half crosswise. Sprinkle each half with salt. Combine bread crumbs, Parmesan cheese, olive oil and basil; mix well. Sprinkle over tomatoes. Bake 15 to 20 minutes or until well heated.

**Herbed Zucchini Strips:**
Cut zucchini into quarters, lengthwise. In a medium saucepan, combine butter or margarine and water; heat to boiling. Add zucchini strips; sprinkle with basil and salt. Cover and cook just until tender, about 10 to 15 minutes.

**Steamed Corn:**
Cut corn into 2- to 3-inch lengths. Add to boiling salted water. Cover. Cook 5 to 8 minutes.

# Green Peppers Stuffed With Mediterranean Rice

*Green peppers cut lengthwise give a new look to a traditional shape.*

1 cup UNCLE BEN'S® CONVERTED® Brand Rice
2-1/2 cups water
1 teaspoon salt
1 tablespoon butter or margarine
1 medium tomato, chopped
6 green onions, chopped
1/3 cup chopped pitted ripe olives

1 clove garlic, minced
2 tablespoons olive oil
1/2 teaspoon salt
3 large green peppers, cut in half lengthwise
Water
1/4 teaspoon salt
1/4 cup grated Parmesan cheese

Cook rice with water, 1 teaspoon salt and butter or margarine according to package directions. Combine tomato, green onions, olives, garlic, olive oil and salt. Mix well. Cover and let stand while rice is cooking. In a large saucepan, parboil green-pepper halves in a small amount of boiling salted water with 1/4 teaspoon salt approximately 5 minutes. Drain peppers well. Stir tomato mixture into hot cooked rice. Fill pepper halves with hot-rice mixture, using about 2/3 cup for each. Sprinkle with Parmesan cheese. Makes 6 servings.

Cook rice according to package directions. Cut peppers in half lengthwise. Chop tomatoes, green onions and olives. Mince garlic.

After parboiling green-pepper halves, stuff each half with about 2/3 cup of hot tomato-rice mixture.

# Artichoke Hearts With Wild Rice

*Drenched with tangy lemon-butter. Mmmm.*

1 (6-oz.) pkg. UNCLE BEN'S®
   Long Grain & Wild Rice
2-1/2 cups water

1 (9-oz.) pkg. frozen artichoke hearts
1/4 cup butter or margarine
1 tablespoon lemon juice

Cook contents of rice and seasoning packets in water according to package directions, omitting butter. Cook artichoke hearts according to package directions; drain well. Melt butter or margarine and combine with lemon juice. Add artichoke hearts to hot cooked rice. Pour lemon-butter over rice and artichokes and mix lightly. Serve immediately. Makes 4 servings.

# Spinach-Broccoli Casserole

*Rice and green vegetables baked in a creamy, cheese-flavored sauce.*

1 (6-oz.) pkg UNCLE BEN'S®
   Long Grain & Wild Rice
2-1/2 cups water
1 tablespoon butter or margarine
1/4 cup butter or margarine
1 cup chopped onion
1 cup sliced celery
1 (10-3/4-oz.) can condensed
   cream-of-mushroom soup
1 (10-3/4-oz.) can condensed
   cream-of-chicken soup

1/2 cup shredded cheddar cheese
1/4 cup diced pimiento
1 (10-oz.) pkg. frozen chopped spinach,
   thawed and drained
1 (10-oz.) pkg frozen chopped broccoli
   thawed and drained
1/4 cup grated Parmesan cheese
Paprika

Preheat oven to 350°F (177°C). Cook contents of rice and seasoning packets with water and 1 tablespoon butter or margarine according to package directions. In a large saucepan, heat 1/4 cup butter or margarine. Add onion and celery. Cook until onion is tender, not brown. Stir in soups, cheddar cheese and pimiento. Arrange half the spinach and broccoli in a 12" x 8" baking dish. Cover with half the rice mixture. Repeat using remaining spinach, broccoli and rice mixture. Cover with aluminum foil, crimping it tightly to edges of dish. Bake 25 minutes. Uncover and sprinkle with Parmesan cheese. Return to oven until hot and bubbly, about 10 minutes. Sprinkle with paprika. Makes 8 servings.

# Tomato-Okra Pilaf

*A sensational vegetable-rice side dish.*

1-1/2 cups UNCLE BEN'S® CONVERTED®
   Brand Rice
3-1/3 cups water
1 tablespoon salt
3 slices bacon, diced

1 small onion, chopped
1 (1-lb.) can stewed tomatoes
1 (10-oz.) pkg. frozen cut okra, thawed
1-1/2 teaspoons salt
Pepper to taste

Cook rice with water and 1 tablespoon salt according to package directions. Cook bacon in a large skillet or Dutch oven until crisp; remove bacon. Add onion to drippings. Cook until tender. Add tomatoes, okra, salt and pepper. Bring to a boil. Reduce heat and cover. Cook about 10 minutes or until okra is tender. Stir cooked rice into tomato-okra mixture. Cover. Cook over low heat until liquid is absorbed, about 5 minutes. Stir in bacon. Makes 8 servings.

# Vegetable-Nut Patties

*Three-in-one: nutritious, meatless and economical.*

1/2 cup chopped celery
1/4 cup chopped onion
2 tablespoons butter or margarine
1/2 cup UNCLE BEN'S® CONVERTED®
   Brand Rice
1-1/3 cups water
1/2 teaspoon salt
1 cup chopped pecans or other nuts

1 cup shredded natural Swiss cheese
2 tablespoons chopped parsley
2 tablespoons chopped pimiento
1 egg, beaten
1/4 cup fine corn-flake crumbs
Fine corn-flake crumbs, for coating patties
Sliced stuffed olives for garnish

Cook celery and onion slowly in butter or margarine until onion is tender, not brown. Stir in rice. Add water and salt. Cover and simmer 20 minutes. Remove from heat. Let stand, covered, until all liquid is absorbed, about 5 minutes. Stir in nuts, cheese, parsley, pimiento, egg and 1/4 cup corn-flake crumbs. Mix well. Shape mixture into 18 patties. Coat patties generously with corn-flake crumbs. Chill until ready to use. Preheat oven to 400°F (204°C). Arrange on baking sheets. Bake until patties are hot, about 8 to 10 minutes. Garnish with sliced stuffed olives. Makes 6 servings.

# How To Make
# Stuffed Artichokes
# With Lemon Butter

Trim artichoke stems so they will sit upright on flat bottoms. Cut off the top third of each artichoke and trim the leaf tips.

To make a hollow for stuffing the artichoke, remove the fuzzy choke with a spoon or melon-ball maker.

Cook artichokes and prepare rice stuffing. Fill artichokes with rice stuffing.

# Stuffed Artichokes With Lemon Butter

*For your most elegant dinners.*

6 fresh artichokes
Boiling salted water
1 (6-oz.) pkg. UNCLE BEN'S®
   Long Grain & Wild Rice
Water

1 (4-oz.) can sliced mushrooms, drained,
   reserve liquid
1 cup melted butter or margarine
1/4 cup lemon juice

Trim stems of artichokes, leaving a flat bottom, so the artichokes will sit upright; cut off top 1/3 of each. With scissors, trim tips of remaining outside leaves. With spoon or melon baller, remove fuzzy choke and enough of center to make generous hollow. In a large saucepan, set artichokes upright in small amount of boiling salted water. Cover. Simmer 30 to 40 minutes or until tender. Drain upside down on paper towels. Keep warm. Add water to reserved mushroom liquid to make 2-1/2 cups liquid. Cook contents of rice and seasoning packets with mushroom liquid according to package directions. Add mushrooms to hot cooked rice. Pile rice into artichokes. Combine melted butter or margarine with lemon juice. Spoon about 1 tablespoon of lemon-butter over each artichoke. Divide remaining lemon-butter among 6 individual cups for dipping artichoke leaves. Makes 6 servings.

# South Seas Rice & Snow Peas

*Crisp, tender snow peas in flavorful rice.*

1 (10-1/2-oz.) can condensed beef broth
Water
2 cups UNCLE BEN'S® QUICK™
   Brand Rice
1 tablespoon vegetable oil
1/2 teaspoon salt
1/2 teaspoon monosodium glutamate,
   if desired

Dash pepper
2 tablespoons vegetable oil
1/2 lb. fresh or 1 (7-oz.) pkg. frozen
   snow peas, thawed
1/2 cup 1-inch-long green-onion strips
1/4 cup coarsely chopped pimiento

Pour beef broth into measuring cup and add water to make 1-2/3 cups. Combine rice, water and broth, 1 tablespoon oil, salt, monosodium glutamate, if desired, and pepper in a large saucepan; mix. Bring to a *vigorous* boil and cover. Simmer until liquid is absorbed, about 5 minutes. Heat 2 tablespoons oil in skillet over high heat. Add snow peas and green onions. Cook and stir for 2 minutes. Add with pimiento to rice; stir. Serve immediately. Makes 4 servings.

# Valencia Rice & Carrots

*Butter and marmalade glaze this sunny orange casserole.*

1/4 cup finely chopped celery
2 tablespoons finely chopped onion
2 tablespoons butter or margarine
2 cups UNCLE BEN'S® QUICK™ Brand Rice
1 cup water
2/3 cup orange juice

1-1/2 teaspoons sugar
1-1/2 teaspoons grated orange peel
1/2 teaspoon salt
2 cups thinly sliced carrots, cooked and drained
1 tablespoon butter or margarine
1/4 cup orange marmalade

Cook celery and onion in 2 tablespoons butter or margarine over low heat until tender. Stir in rice, water, orange juice, sugar, orange peel and salt. Bring to a *vigorous* boil and cover. Simmer 5 minutes or until liquid is absorbed. Heat carrots. Add 1 tablespoon butter or margarine to hot carrots and mix carefully. Add marmalade and again mix carefully. Spoon rice into heated serving dish or casserole. Spoon carrots around edge. Makes 4 to 6 servings.

# Creamed Onions in Wild Rice Ring

*Add variety to your meals with a different vegetable combination every time.*

2 (6-oz.) pkgs. UNCLE BEN'S® Long Grain & Wild Rice
2-1/2 cups water
1 tablespoon butter or margarine
1/4 cup butter or margarine
1/4 cup flour
1 teaspoon salt
1-1/2 cups milk

1 cup half and half
1-1/2 to 2 lbs. tiny white fresh onions, cooked and drained, or 2 (1-lb.) jars whole onions, drained
1 cup 1-in.-long green-onion strips
2 tablespoons diced pimiento
1 cup shredded Monterey Jack cheese

Generously butter a 6-cup ring mold. Cook contents of rice and seasoning packets with water and 1 tablespoon butter or margarine according to package directions. In a large saucepan, melt butter or margarine. Blend in flour and salt. Add milk and half and half. Cook, stirring constantly, until thickened and smooth. Add white onions, green onions and pimiento; heat thoroughly. Fold cheese into cooked rice. Spoon into buttered ring mold. Let stand about 15 minutes. To keep warm, cover with aluminum foil; let stand in 250°F (121°C) oven. Unmold on heated serving plate. Serve with creamed onions. If desired, onions may be placed in small dish that fits into center of mold. Makes 12 servings.

# Cantonese Rice & Asparagus

*Pungent Chinese rice—a gourmet's complement to spare ribs.*

3 tablespoons vegetable oil
1 small clove garlic, sliced
1 lb. fresh asparagus, cut diagonally
   into 2- to 3-inch lengths
2 cups UNCLE BEN'S® QUICK™
   Brand Rice
1/2 teaspoon salt

1/2 teaspoon ground ginger
1/2 teaspoon sugar
1/4 teaspoon monosodium glutamate,
   if desired
1 (13-3/4-oz.) can chicken broth
2 teaspoons soy sauce

In a large skillet, heat oil and garlic over moderately high heat until garlic is lightly browned. Remove garlic and add asparagus. Cook, stirring constantly, for 1 minute. Add rice, salt, ginger, sugar and monosodium glutamate, if desired. Mix. Stir in broth and soy sauce. Bring to a *vigorous* boil. Cover. Simmer until liquid is absorbed, about 5 minutes. Stir before serving. Makes 4 servings.

# Spinach & Brown Rice Greek-Style

*Just the right touch for an international buffet.*

1 cup UNCLE BEN'S® Brown Rice
2-2/3 cups water
1 teaspoon salt
1 tablespoon butter or margarine
2 tablespoons olive oil
2 medium onions, chopped
1 clove garlic, minced

1 (10-oz.) pkg. frozen chopped spinach,
   thawed and drained
1/2 teaspoon salt
1 medium tomato, chopped
1 tablespoon lemon juice
1/2 teaspoon grated lemon peel
1 cup shredded Swiss cheese

Cook rice with water, 1 teaspoon salt and butter or margarine according to package directions. Heat oil in a large skillet. Add onions and garlic. Cook until onion is tender, but not brown. Add spinach and salt; stir. Cook until spinach is tender, about 5 minutes. Stir in hot cooked rice, tomato, lemon juice and lemon peel. Sprinkle with cheese. Makes 6 servings.

# Zucchini With Brown Rice Stuffing

*Savory herb stuffing gives vegetables new appeal.*

1/2 cup UNCLE BEN'S® Brown Rice
1-3/4 cups water
1/2 teaspoon salt
1/2 tablespoon butter or margarine
4 medium zucchini
2 tablespoons butter or margarine
1/4 cup finely chopped onion

1 medium tomato, chopped and drained
2 tablespoons chopped parsley
1/4 teaspoon basil
1/4 teaspoon leaf thyme
3/4 teaspoon salt
2 tablespoons grated Parmesan cheese

Preheat oven to 350°F (177°C). Cook brown rice with water, 1/2 teaspoon salt and 1/2 tablespoon butter or margarine according to package directions. Trim off ends of zucchini; cut in half lengthwise. Scoop out center leaving a 1/4-inch shell on each. Finely chop scooped-out centers of zucchini. In a medium skillet melt 2 tablespoons butter or margarine. Add onion, tomato and chopped zucchini. Cook until moisture is evaporated, about 10 minutes. Add parsley, basil, thyme and 1/4 teaspoon of salt. Stir mixture into cooked brown rice. Cool slightly. Sprinkle zucchini shells with remaining 1/2 teaspoon salt. Fill with brown rice mixture. Place in a shallow 2-quart casserole. Cover tightly. Bake until hot, about 20 minutes. Uncover. Sprinkle with Parmeasan cheese. Return to oven to melt cheese, about 5 to 8 minutes. Makes 8 servings.

# Side Dishes

UNCLE BEN'S® Rice goes with everything. It brings out flavors and adds traditional texture. The next time you stuff a turkey, chicken or Cornish game hen, try delicious Holiday Stuffing. Everyone's favorite is Bacon-Lettuce-Tomato Rice. Rice absorbs sauces and gravies, and is a good accompaniment for highly seasoned sauces. Top Brown Rice Pilaf with meat and gravy. Or mound colorful Fruited Brown Rice beside fried chicken. With UNCLE BEN'S® recipes you'll find new ways to add color and flavor to rice side dishes, using fruit and vegetable juices, tomato sauce, canned sauces, syrups and herbs.

*Festive Easter Feast*
    Rock Cornish Game Hens
\*  Holiday Stuffing
    Asparagus, Lemon Butter
    Fruit Salad
    Easter Chocolate Mousse

*South of the Border*
    Broiled Steak
\*  Mexican Fire & Ice Casserole
    Guacamole Salad
    Tostadas
    Caramel Custard

*Dinner Winner*
    Roast Leg of Lamb
\*  Emerald Rice
    Marinated Cooked Carrots,
    Mushrooms, Celery
    Key Lime Pie

*Barbecue on the Patio*
    Hamburger Patties
\*  Bacon-Lettuce-Tomato Rice
    Corn on the Cob
    Apple Turnovers

*Holiday Party Gala*
    Sherry Glazed Ham
\*  Orange Holiday Rice
    Broccoli & Creamed Onions
    Pumpkin Ice Cream

*Neighbors Gather*
    Fried Chicken
\*  Fruited Brown Rice
    Peas and Mushrooms
    Mixed Greens
    Orange Sherbet in Orange Shells

*These recipes are in this section.*

# Toasted Almond Rice

*The ideal accompaniment for roast lamb or sautéed chicken.*

1-1/2 tablespoons butter or margarine
1 teaspoon curry powder
1 cup sliced celery
1 small onion, diced

1 (6-oz.) pkg. UNCLE BEN'S®
  Long Grain & Wild Rice
2-1/2 cups water
1 cup slivered almonds

Preheat oven to 400°F (204°C). In a large saucepan, melt butter or margarine. Add curry powder. Cook 1 minute, stirring constantly, being careful not to burn the mixture. Add celery and onion. Cook, stirring constantly, 3 minutes. Add contents of rice and seasoning packets and water. Bring to a boil and cover. Simmer until all liquid is absorbed, about 25 minutes. Spread almonds in a large flat pan. Bake for 5 minutes, or until toasted. Or toast almonds in a heavy skillet, stirring frequently. Stir into hot cooked rice. Makes 6 to 8 servings.

# Brown Rice Pilaf

*Start with this basic recipe and go on to your favorite pilaf.*

1 cup UNCLE BEN'S® Brown Rice
1 (13-3/4 oz.) can chicken broth
Water

1 cup sliced celery
1/2 cup chopped onion
1/4 cup butter or margarine

Cook brown rice with chicken broth and water to make 2-2/3 cups liquid according to package directions, omitting butter. In a small skillet, cook celery and onion in butter or margarine until onion is tender, not brown. Stir into hot cooked rice. Makes 5 to 6 servings.

**Variations:**

To make Almond Raisin Pilaf, add 1/2 cup seedless raisins to liquid with rice. Stir 1/2 cup toasted chopped almonds into hot cooked rice.

To make Herb Mushroom Pilaf, cook 1 cup sliced fresh mushrooms with celery and onion. Add 2 tablespoons chopped parsley, 1/2 teaspoon each of marjoram and thyme and stir into hot cooked rice.

To make Brown Rice Risotto, add 1 cup cooked green peas and 1/2 cup finely diced cooked ham to cooked celery and onion mixture. Heat through. Add to rice with 1/4 cup grated or shredded Parmesan cheese.

To make Nutted Pilaf, omit celery and onion and add 1/4 teaspoon each: cinnamon, allspice, mace and cloves to broth and rice before cooking. Brown 1/4 cup chopped walnuts and 1/4 cup raisins in 1 tablespoon butter or margarine until raisins are puffed. Blend into rice.

# Fruited Brown Rice

*Brown-rice goodness with honey and fruit.*

2-2/3 cups water
1 cup UNCLE BEN'S® Brown Rice
1 cup chopped, peeled raw apple
1/4 cup chopped onion
1 teaspoon salt

1/2 cup slivered almonds
2 tablespoons butter or margarine
1/2 cup chopped soft dried apricots
2 tablespoons honey

Bring water to a boil. Stir in brown rice, apple, onion and salt. Bring to a boil. Cover tightly. Simmer until all water is absorbed, about 50 minutes. Lightly brown almonds in butter or margarine. Stir almond-butter mixture into hot cooked rice. Stir in apricots and honey. Makes 5 to 6 servings.

# Honeyed Apples in Brown Rice

*Sweet apple rice can be a light meal by itself.*

1 cup UNCLE BEN'S® Brown Rice
2-2/3 cups water
1 teaspoon salt
1 tablespoon butter or margarine
2 tablespoons butter or margarine

2 medium cooking apples, cored and chopped
1/4 cup honey
1/2 cup coarsely chopped walnuts
1/2 cup sliced celery
1 teaspoon grated orange peel

Cook rice with water, salt and 1 tablespoon butter or margarine according to package directions. In a large skillet, melt 2 tablespoons butter or margarine. Add apple and honey. Cook and stir carefully until apples are tender but still hold their shape, about 5 to 8 minutes. Stir in hot cooked rice, walnuts and celery. Sprinkle with orange peel. Makes 6 servings.

# Tomato-Rice Ring Italian-Style

*Fresh, buttery vegetables framed with colorful rice.*

1 large tomato, thinly sliced
1 cup UNCLE BEN'S® CONVERTED®
  Brand Rice
2-1/2 cups water
1 teaspoon salt
1 tablespoon butter or margarine
2 tablespoons olive oil
1/2 lb. green beans, cut in 1-in. lengths

1 medium onion, chopped
1 clove garlic, minced
2 medium zucchini, cut in 1/4-in. slices
2 medium yellow squash, cut in 1/4-in. slices
1 teaspoon salt
1/2 teaspoon oregano
2 tablespoons butter or margarine
2 tablespoons grated Parmesan cheese

Butter a 4-1/2-cup ring mold and line bottom with tomato slices. Cook rice with water, 1 teaspoon salt and 1 tablespoon butter or margarine according to package directions. In a large skillet, heat olive oil. Add green beans, onion and garlic. Cover. Cook slowly 10 minutes. Add zucchini, yellow squash, 1 teaspoon salt and oregano. Cover. Cook until vegetables are just tender, about 10 minutes. Add 2 tablespoons butter or margarine. Heat just until melted. When rice is cooked, stir in cheese. Lightly spoon rice mixture into prepared ring mold. Let stand about 5 minutes. Turn out by inverting on a serving plate. Fill center of rice ring with vegetables. Makes 6 servings.

**Line the bottom of a buttered ring mold with tomato slices.**

**Spoon cooked rice onto tomato layer. Do not pack the rice down.**

# Southwestern Rice

*Serve a Mexican-style supper around this spicy rice.*

2 tablespoons butter or margarine
1/3 cup chopped onion
1/4 cup chili pepper, chopped
1 cup UNCLE BEN'S® CONVERTED®
   Brand Rice
1 (10-1/2-oz.) can condensed beef
   broth or chicken consommé

1 soup-can water
3/4 teaspoon cumin seeds
3/4 teaspoon salt
1 teaspoon Worcestershire sauce
Chopped black olives
Avocado slices for garnish, if desired

In a large saucepan, melt butter or margarine. Add onion, chili pepper and rice. Cook, stirring often until lightly browned. Add broth or consommé, water, cumin seeds, salt and Worcestershire sauce. Bring to a boil and cover tightly. Simmer 20 minutes. Remove from heat. Let stand, covered, until all liquid is absorbed, about 5 minutes. Sprinkle with olives. Garnish with avocado slices. Makes 4 servings.

# Cranberry Stuffing en Casserole

*Holiday-perfect stuffing.*

1 (6-oz.) pkg. UNCLE BEN'S®
   Long Grain & Wild Rice
2-1/2 cups water
1 tablespoon butter or margarine
1 cup raw cranberries

1 cup sliced celery
1/2 cup sugar
1/2 cup chopped salted cashews
1 teaspoon grated orange peel

Preheat oven to 350°F (177°C). Cook contents of rice and seasoning packets with water and butter or margarine according to package directions. Stir cranberries into cooked rice. Heat, uncovered, until berries begin to pop, about 5 minutes. Stir in celery, sugar, cashews and orange peel. Spoon into a shallow 1-1/2 quart casserole. Cover tightly. Place in oven and heat thoroughly 30 to 40 minutes. Makes 6 to 8 servings.

### Variation:
To use as stuffing for 5 to 7 (1-pound) Cornish game hens, wash, drain and dry hens. Sprinkle cavities of each hen with 1/4 teaspoon salt. Spoon rice mixture loosely into cavities, using about 3/4 cup for each. Close cavities with small metal skewers. Place hens, breast side up, on rack in a shallow roasting pan. Brush well with melted butter or margarine. Bake, uncovered, in 350°F (177°C) oven until tender and leg joints move easily, about 1 hour. Brush several times during cooking with melted butter.

# Sherried-Mushroom Wild Rice

*Something special—and easy, too.*

1 (6-oz.) pkg. UNCLE BEN'S®
   Long Grain & Wild Rice
2-1/2 cups water
1 small onion, chopped
1/4 cup butter or margarine
1/2 lb. fresh mushrooms, sliced

1/4 cup dry sherry
1/4 teaspoon salt
1 cup sliced celery
1 (2-oz.) jar sliced pimiento,
   drained

Cook contents of rice and seasoning packets with water according to package directions, omitting butter. In a medium skillet, cook onion in butter or margarine until tender, but not brown. Add mushrooms. Cook until tender, about 5 minutes. Add sherry and salt. Cook until liquid evaporates, stirring frequently. Stir mushroom mixture, celery and pimiento into hot cooked rice. Heat through. Makes 6 servings.

# Apple-Walnut Wild Rice

*Holiday rice—full of surprises!*

1 (6-oz.) pkg. UNCLE BEN'S®
   Long Grain & Wild Rice
2-1/4 cups water
1 tablespoon butter or margarine
1/4 cup Madeira
2 tablespoons butter or margarine

2 medium tart cooking apples,
   coarsely chopped
2 tablespoons brown sugar
1 cup sliced celery
1/2 cup chopped walnuts
1/4 cup diced candied citron

Cook contents of rice and seasoning packets with water, 1 tablespoon butter or margarine and Madeira according to package directions. In a small saucepan, melt 2 tablespoons butter or margarine. Add chopped apples and sprinkle with brown sugar. Cook until apple pieces are just tender, but still hold their shape, stirring frequently. Stir apple mixture, celery, walnuts and candied citron into hot cooked rice. Heat through. Serve with duck. Makes 6 servings.

# Raisin Rice

*Has a sweet, mellow flavor. Delicious with pork or meat loaf.*

1 cup UNCLE BEN'S® CONVERTED®
  Brand Rice
1/2 cup raisins
3 tablespoons sugar
1/2 teaspoon grated lemon peel

1/2 teaspoon turmeric
1/2 teaspoon salt
1 tablespoon butter or margarine
2-1/2 cups boiling water

Preheat oven to 350°F (177°C). Place all ingredients in a 3-quart baking dish. Stir to mix thoroughly. Cover. Bake until liquid is absorbed and rice is tender, about 35 minutes. Makes 6 to 8 servings.


# Cheese-Rice Bake

*Makes a hamburger supper extra special.*

1 (6-oz.) pkg. UNCLE BEN'S®
  Long Grain & Wild Rice
2-1/2 cups water
1 tablespoon butter or margarine
3 cups sliced zucchini
2 tablespoons chopped green chilies
1-1/2 cups shredded Monterey Jack cheese
  (3/4 lb.)

1 large tomato, cut in 6 slices
1 cup dairy sour cream
1/2 teaspoon oregano
1/2 teaspoon garlic salt
1/2 cup shredded Monterey Jack cheese
  (1/4 lb.)
2 tablespoons chopped parsley

Preheat oven to 375°F (191°C). Cook contents of rice and seasoning packets with water and butter or margarine according to package directions. Mix together cooked rice, zucchini, green chilies and 1-1/2 cups cheese. Spread mixture in a 12" x 8" baking dish. Cover with aluminum foil, crimping it tightly to edges of dish. Bake 40 minutes. Remove from oven and remove foil. Top with tomato slices. Mix together sour cream, oregano and garlic salt. Cover tomatoes with sour-cream mixture. Sprinkle with remaining 1/2-cup of cheese. Broil until cheese just melts and lightly browns. Garnish with chopped parsley. Makes 6 servings.

# Persian Rice

*For rice adventurers!*

1 (11-oz.) can mandarin-orange segments
1/2 cup crushed pineapple
Water
1 (6-1/4-oz.) pkg. UNCLE BEN'S® Fast
   Cooking Long Grain & Wild Rice

2 tablespoons butter or margarine
2 tablespoons currants or chopped raisins
1 tablespoon chopped green onions with tops

Drain mandarin-orange segments and pineapple; reserve liquid. Add water to fruit liquid to make 2 cups. Cook contents of rice and seasoning packets with fruit liquid, water and butter or margarine according to package directions. Fold in currants or raisins, orange segments and pineapple. Just before serving, fold in chopped onions. Makes 6 to 8 servings.

# Polynesian Orange Rice

*Here's one way to have dessert with your meal!*

1 cup UNCLE BEN'S® CONVERTED®
   Brand Rice
2-1/2 cups water
1 teaspoon salt
1 tablespoon butter or margarine
1 cup whipping cream
2 (11-oz.) cans mandarin orange
   segments, drained

3/4 cup finely diced celery
1/2 cup chopped walnuts or pecans
1/2 cup chopped chutney
1/3 cup flaked coconut
1/2 teaspoon salt

Preheat oven to 350°F (177°C). Lightly butter a 12" x 8" baking dish. Cook rice with water, 1 teaspoon salt and butter or margarine according to package directions. Whip cream until stiff. Fold in orange segments, celery, nuts, chutney, coconut and 1/2 teaspoon salt. Spread rice over bottom of buttered baking dish. Spoon whipped-cream mixture evenly over top. Bake until heated, about 30 minutes. Serve with lamb or pork. Makes 6 servings.

Variations:
Substitute 4 cups cooked UNCLE BEN'S® QUICK™ Brand Rice for cooked UNCLE BEN'S® CONVERTED® Brand Rice.

Add 1 (13-1/2-oz.) can pineapple tidbits, well drained.

# How To Make Chinese Fried Rice

Cook the eggs, stirring slightly. Remove from the pan in one flat piece and lay the piece on a plate to cool.

In the same skillet, cook the onions and meat in vegetable oil. Add rice and stir.

Stir in egg strips and heat.

# Chinese Fried Rice

*Here's competition for Chinese restaurants.*

1-1/2 cups UNCLE BEN'S® CONVERTED®
  Brand Rice
3-1/4 cups water
1-1/2 teaspoons salt
3 tablespoons vegetable oil
2 eggs, beaten
1/2 cup sliced green onions, with tops
1/2 cup cooked pork, chicken or beef,
  cut in short julienne strips

1/4 cup cooked ham, cut in short
  julienne strips
2 tablespoons soy sauce
1/2 teaspoon sugar
1/2 teaspoon salt
1/4 teaspoon monosodium glutamate,
  if desired

Cook rice with water and 1-1/2 teaspoon salt according to package directions, omitting butter; chill thoroughly. Heat 1/2 of the oil in a large skillet. Add eggs. Cook 1 minute, stirring slightly. Remove from pan. Spread on a flat plate in a thin layer and cool. Cut into thin strips. Add remaining oil to skillet and heat. Add onions and meat. Cook and stir just until heated. Add cold rice; stir well to coat rice with oil. Stir in eggs and remaining ingredients; heat thoroughly. Makes 8 servings.

# Emerald Rice

*A delicious protein-filled luncheon dish.*

1/2 cup UNCLE BEN'S® CONVERTED®
  Brand Rice
1-1/3 cups water
1/2 teaspoon salt
1/2 tablespoon butter or margarine

3 eggs, separated
1 cup shredded sharp Cheddar cheese (1/2 lb.)
1/2 cup minced fresh parsley
2 tablespoons chopped onion
1/2 cup butter or margarine, melted

Preheat oven to 350°F (177°C). Cook rice with water, salt and 1/2 tablespoon butter or margarine according to package directions for half the basic recipe. Beat egg yolks until light and fluffy. Combine rice, cheese, parsley, onion, butter or margarine and beaten egg yolks. Beat egg whites until they hold soft peaks. Fold into rice mixture. Pour into 1-1/2-quart casserole or soufflé dish. Bake until done, 25 to 30 minutes. Table knife inserted in center of casserole will come out clean when done. Makes 4 to 6 servings.

# Red Beans & Rice

*Spicy rice 'n beans—try it over a campfire.*

1 (1-lb.) can kidney or red beans
Water
1 cup UNCLE BEN'S® CONVERTED®
  Brand Rice

1-1/2 cups sliced onion
1 teaspoon garlic salt
1 teaspoon salt
1 teaspoon chili powder

Drain kidney beans; reserve juice. Add water as needed to make 2-1/2 cups liquid. In a large skillet, combine kidney beans, liquid, rice, onion, garlic salt, salt and chili powder. Stir. Bring to a boil and cover. Simmer 20 minutes. Remove from heat. Let stand, covered, until all liquid is absorbed, about 5 minutes. Makes 4 to 6 servings.

### Variations:

Sprinkle with 1 cup shredded Cheddar cheese at end of 20 minutes cooking time. Cover and let stand to melt cheese and absorb liquid.

Substitute black-eyed peas for kidney or red beans.

# Monterey Brown Rice

*Bake nutritious brown rice with melted cheese and crisp vegetables.*

1-1/2 cups UNCLE BEN'S®
  Brown Rice
1-1/2 teaspoon salt
2 chicken-bouillon cubes, crumbled
1 cup thinly sliced celery
1/2 cup sliced onion

1/4 cup chopped green pepper
1/4 cup butter or margarine
3-1/2 cups boiling water
1 cup shredded Monterey Jack cheese
1 cup sliced pitted ripe olives
2 tablespoons chopped parsley

Preheat oven to 350°F (177°C). Place brown rice, salt and bouillon cubes in a 2-quart casserole. In a small skillet, cook celery, onion and green pepper in butter or margarine until onion is tender, not brown. Add to brown rice in casserole. Stir in boiling water and mix well. Cover tightly. Bake until rice is tender and liquid is absorbed, about 1 hour. Stir in cheese, olives and parsley. Cover. Return to oven to heat, about 5 minutes. Makes 7 to 8 servings.

# Monterey Risotto

*Adds style to any meal.*

2 tablespoons butter or margarine
1 cup sliced fresh mushrooms
1/4 cup chopped onion
1 cup UNCLE BEN'S® CONVERTED®
   Brand Rice

2 cups chicken broth
1/2 cup dry white wine
1 teaspoon salt
1 cup shredded Monterey Jack cheese

In a large saucepan, melt butter or margarine. Add mushrooms and onion. Sauté until golden. Add rice, chicken broth, wine and salt; stir. Bring to a boil and cover. Simmer 20 minutes. Remove from heat. Let stand, covered, until all liquid is absorbed, about 5 minutes. Fold in cheese. Makes 6 servings.

# Holiday Stuffing

*Don't wait for a holiday to try this savory stuffing.*

2 (6-oz.) pkg. UNCLE BEN'S®
   Long Grain & Wild Rice
4 cups water
1 tablespoon butter or margarine
2 diced carrots

1/2 lb. brown and serve pork-sausage
   links, sliced
1/4 cup chopped onion
1/2 cup celery leaves
1/2 cup sliced mushrooms

Cook contents of rice and seasoning packets with water, butter or margarine and diced carrots according to package directions. In a large skillet, brown pork-sausage-link slices. Add onion, celery leaves and mushrooms. Cook 3 minutes. Toss rice gently with pork-sausage mixture to mix well. Use about 1/2-cup rice mixture per pound of bird. Makes enough to stuff one 8 to 10-lb. turkey, or two 4-lb. ducklings, or one 6-lb. capon, plus extra to bake and serve separately.

Variation:
Place stuffing in a lightly greased, 2-quart casserole. Bake, covered at 325°F (163°C) 25 minutes.

# Risi e Bisi

*Try this famous Italian Rice.*

1/4 cup butter or margarine
1/2 cup chopped onion
2 cups UNCLE BEN'S® QUICK™
   Brand Rice
1 (10-oz.) pkg. frozen peas, thawed

1/4 teaspoon salt
1 (13-3/4-oz.) can chicken broth
1/2 cup finely diced cooked ham
1/4 cup grated or shredded Parmesan cheese

In a large saucepan, melt butter or margarine. Add onion and cook until tender, but not brown. Add rice, peas and salt; mix well. Stir in broth. Bring to a *vigorous* boil and cover. Simmer until all liquid is absorbed, about 5 minutes. Add ham and 3 tablespoons of the cheese. Stir and heat slightly. Sprinkle with remaining cheese. Makes 4 servings.

**Variation:**
Substitute 1 (6-oz.) package UNCLE BEN'S® Long Grain & Wild Rice for UNCLE BEN'S® QUICK™ Brand Rice, and 2-1/2 cups water for chicken broth. Stir in peas, ham and cheese. Cover and let stand for 3 minutes.

# Orange Holiday Rice

*Serve in hollowed-out orange shells for a gala effect.*

2-1/4 cups water or chicken broth
1 cup UNCLE BEN'S® CONVERTED®
   Brand Rice
1/2 teaspoon salt
1/4 cup butter or margarine

Juice of 1 orange
Grated peel of 1 orange
1/2 cup fresh orange sections
1/2 cup salted roasted cashew nuts

Preheat oven to 350°F (177°C). In a 1-1/2 quart casserole, combine water or chicken broth, rice, salt, butter or margarine and juice of 1 orange. Cover. Bake until rice is tender and all liquid has been absorbed, about 45 minutes to 1 hour. Stir in orange peel. Cover and return to oven for 10 minutes. Just before serving, toss rice with orange sections and cashew nuts. Correct seasoning if necessary. Serve with turkey or chicken. Makes 6 servings.

# Bacon-Lettuce-Tomato Rice

*Rice magic turns sandwich ingredients into a delicious luncheon dish.*

1/4-lb. sliced bacon, diced
1 cup UNCLE BEN'S® CONVERTED®
  Brand Rice
2-1/2 cups water
1 teaspoon salt

1/2 cup dairy sour cream
1 teaspoon salt
2 medium tomatoes, diced
1/2 medium head lettuce, shredded
2 tablespoons chopped green chilies

In large skillet or 2-quart saucepan, fry bacon until crisp. Remove bacon bits from pan. Pour off all but 2 tablespoons bacon drippings. Add rice, water and 1 teaspoon salt to drippings; stir. Bring to a boil. Cover and simmer about 20 minutes. Remove from heat. Let stand, covered, until all liquid is absorbed, about 5 minutes. Stir in sour cream and 1 teaspoon salt. Lightly stir in tomatoes, lettuce and green chilies. Heat through. Sprinkle with bacon bits. Serve immediately. Makes 6 servings.

# Mexican Fire & Ice Casserole

*Match hot chilies against sour cream and enjoy a tasty bout.*

3-1/2 cups *cooked* and chilled UNCLE BEN'S®
  CONVERTED® Brand Rice
1 (3-1/2-oz.) can pitted ripe olives,
  drained and sliced
1 cup dairy sour cream

1/2 cup shredded Monterey Jack cheese
1/4 cup mayonnaise
3 tablespoons peeled and chopped
  roasted green chilies
2 to 3 tablespoons sliced green onion

Preheat oven to 350°F (177°C). Combine cooked rice, olives, sour cream, cheese, mayonnaise, green chilies and green onion. Mix well. Spoon into a 1-quart casserole. Cover. Bake until hot, about 25 minutes. Serve with meat. Makes 4 to 6 servings.

**Variation:**
Substitute 3/4 teaspoon chili powder for green chilies.

# Oriental Wild Rice

*Love that water-chestnut crunch!*

1 (13-3/4-oz.) can chicken broth
Water
1 tablespoon butter or margarine
1 (6-oz.) pkg. UNCLE BEN'S®
   Long Grain & Wild Rice

1 (8-oz.) can water chestnuts,
   drained and chopped
4 green onions, sliced
1 (2-oz.) jar sliced pimiento, drained
1/4 teaspoon salt

Combine chicken broth with enough water to make 2-1/2 cups liquid. Place in a large saucepan with butter or margarine. Stir in contents of rice and seasoning packets. Cook according to package directions about 25 minutes. Stir in water chestnuts, green onions, pimiento and salt. Heat through. Makes 6 servings.

# Rice a la Grecque

*A superlative recipe.*

2 tablespoons butter or margarine
1 cup chopped onions
2-1/2 cups UNCLE BEN'S®
   QUICK™ Brand Rice
2 cups chicken broth

2/3 cup green peas
2/3 cup golden raisins
1/4 teaspoon salt
1/3 cup grated Parmesan cheese

In medium skillet, melt butter or margarine. Add onions and cook until soft. Stir in rice, broth, peas, raisins and salt. Bring to a *vigorous* boil and cover. Simmer until all liquid is absorbed, about 5 minutes. Stir in cheese. Serve hot. Makes 6 servings.

**Variation:**
Omit peas and Parmesan cheese. Add 2 tablespoons cut-up mint leaves and 1 teaspoon grated lemon peel.

# Meats

You can put meat and rice together in such a variety of ways that you can serve a different meat-rice dish almost every night this month. For a starter, please your family with tasty Baked Stroganoff Meatballs. Then try Burgundy Short Ribs with Chili Rice—a hearty, zesty meal. If the weather allows, cook Shish Kebabs on the patio and serve with Buttery Mint Rice. When you want a gourmet-style evening meal but you're limited in time, whip up Ham in Orange-Mustard Sauce. These recipes from UNCLE BEN'S® kitchens are so delicious that once won't be enough. Your family will ask for them over and over again.

### Dinner In A Hurry
* Ham In Orange-Mustard Sauce
  Broccoli
  Green Salad, Zippy Dressing
  Pound Cake, Fruit Sauce

### Supper's On The Patio
* Shish Kebabs & Buttery Mint Rice
  Creamed Peas
  Fresh Spinach Salad,
  Lemon Dressing
  Brownies

### Man-Pleaser
* Burgundy Short Ribs With
    Chili Rice
  Cauliflower Au Gratin
  Cole Slaw
  Chocolate Cake

### A Touch of France
* Lamb Chops & Rice Niçoise
  Buttered Peas & Tiny Onions
  Tossed Green Salad
  French Bread
  Pears Helene

### Luncheon Party
* Reuben Croquettes
  Buttered Asparagus
  Green Salad,
  Oil & Vinegar Dressing
  Rolls, Butter
  Strawberry Soufflé

### Special Dinner for the Family
* Baked Stroganoff Meatballs
  Sautéed Green Beans
  Sliced Tomatoes & Onion Salad
  Baked Apples

*These recipes are in this section.*

# Pork Tenderloin Jardiniere

*Festive layers of succulent pork and garden vegetables.*

2 (3/4-lb.) pork tenderloins
Seasoned salt to taste
2 medium onions
2 medium tomatoes
1 large green pepper
Seasoned salt to taste

1 cup shredded sharp Cheddar cheese
Paprika
1 (6-oz.) pkg. UNCLE BEN'S®
    Long Grain & Wild Rice
1 (9-oz.) pkg. frozen peas

Preheat oven to 350°F (177°C). Split tenderloins lengthwise almost, but not quite through; and open. Sprinkle with seasoned salt. Arrange on rack in shallow pan. Slice onions, tomatoes, and seeded pepper 1/4-inch thick. Place a layer of each on meat, ending with overlapping green pepper slices on top. Sprinkle with seasoned salt. Cover loosely with foil. Bake 1 hour. About 25 minutes before meat is done, cook contents of rice and seasoning packets with water and butter or margarine according to package directions. Cook and drain frozen peas. Combine rice and peas; keep warm. Uncover meat. Bake 10 minutes. Sprinkle top with cheese and paprika. Bake 5 minutes longer. Cut each tenderloin carefully into 3 servings. Serve with rice mixture. Makes 6 servings.

# Pork Adobo

*A tender meat stew from the Philippine Islands.*

2 lbs. boneless lean pork,
    cut in 1-in. cubes
1 tablespoon vegetable oil
3/4 cup water
2 cloves garlic, minced
1 bay leaf
1 teaspoon salt
2 tablespoons flour
2 teaspoons chili powder
1/2 teaspoon cinnamon
1/8 teaspoon ground cloves

1-1/4 cups water
2 tablespoons vinegar
2 tablespoons brown sugar
1 cup UNCLE BEN'S® CONVERTED®
    Brand Rice
2-1/2 cups water
1 teaspoon salt
1 tablespoon butter or margarine
1 cup sliced celery
1 medium avocado, peeled and sliced

In a large skillet, heat oil. Add pork cubes and brown on all sides. Add 3/4 cup water, garlic, bay leaf and salt. Cover. Cook over low heat until meat is tender, about 1 hour. Remove meat from pan; keep warm. Remove bay leaf and discard. Stir flour, chili powder, cinnamon and cloves into pan drippings. Heat and stir several minutes, being careful not to burn. Add 1-1/4 cups water, vinegar and brown sugar. Cook until thickened, stirring constantly. Skim off any excess fat. Return meat to sauce and cover. Simmer to blend flavors, about 10 minutes. Cook rice with 2-1/2 cups water, 1 teaspoon salt and butter or margarine according to package directions. Stir celery into hot cooked rice. Serve pork over rice, garnish with avocado. Makes 6 servings.

# Thursday's Wild Beef & Vegetable Loaf

*Great family fare!*

1-1/2 lbs. lean ground beef
2 medium carrots, shredded
1 small onion, finely chopped
2 eggs
1 cup soft bread crumbs
1/2 cup tomato juice
1 tablespoon Worcestershire sauce

1-1/2 teaspoons salt
1/8 teaspoon pepper
1/4 cup barbecue sauce or catsup
1 (6-oz.) pkg. UNCLE BEN'S®
   Long Grain & Wild Rice
2-1/2 cups water
1 tablespoon butter or margarine

Preheat oven to 350°F (177°C). Combine beef, carrots, onion, eggs, bread crumbs, tomato juice, Worcestershire sauce, salt and pepper. Mix well. Press into an 8-1/2" x 4-1/2" x 2-5/8" loaf pan. Bake until meat is done, about 1 hour and 10 minutes. Cook contents of rice and seasoning packets with water and butter or margarine according to package directions. Ten minutes before end of meat loaf's baking time, spoon barbecue sauce or catsup over meat loaf and finish baking. Serve with rice. Makes 6 servings.

# Fruited Pork Chops

*Enjoy a sweet-sour sauce over tender pork chops.*

2 tablespoons butter or margarine
8 pork chops
1 teaspoon salt
1/4 teaspoon ground ginger
2 tablespoons water
1 cup UNCLE BEN'S® CONVERTED®
   Brand Rice

2-1/2 cups water
1 teaspoon salt
1 tablespoon butter or margarine
Pineapple Sauce, see below

*Pineapple Sauce:*
1 (5-1/4-oz.) can pineapple chunks
1/3 cup brown sugar, firmly packed
2 tablespoons cornstarch
1/3 cup vinegar

2 teaspoons soy sauce
1/4 teaspoon salt
3/4 cup seedless raisins

In a large skillet, melt butter or margarine. Add pork chops. Brown on both sides. Sprinkle with 1 teaspoon salt and ginger. Add water and cover. Cook slowly until meat is fork tender, about 45 minutes. Cook rice with water, 1 teaspoon salt and 1 tablespoon butter or margarine according to package directions. Spoon Pineapple Sauce over pork chops. Cook slowly to glaze well, about 10 minutes. Serve pork chops and sauce over hot cooked rice. Makes 6 to 8 servings.

**Pineapple Sauce:**
Drain pineapple chunks; reserve syrup. Add water to syrup to make 1 cup liquid. Combine liquid, brown sugar, cornstarch, vinegar, soy sauce and 1/4 teaspoon salt. Mix well. Cook, stirring constantly, until clear and thickened. Stir in raisins and pineapple chunks.

# Spring Pork With Rice Loaf

*Orange marmalade makes the gravy.*

2 pork tenderloins (about 3 to 4 lbs.)
1/4 cup flour
2 teaspoons salt
2 tablespoons butter or margarine
1 cup celery, sliced
1 small onion, sliced
1/4 cup dry white wine

1/4 cup water
2 tablespoons orange marmalade
2 tablespoons chopped parsley
2 (6-oz.) pkgs. UNCLE BEN'S®
　　Long Grain & Wild Rice
5 cups chicken stock

Lightly oil a 9" x 5" x 3" loaf pan or 6-cup mold. Cut pork tenderloins into slices 1-inch thick. Combine flour and salt. Dip pork slices in flour and salt to coat all sides. In a large skillet, sauté in butter or margarine until browned on all sides. Push to one side. Add celery and onion and sauté 3 minutes. Add wine and water. Mix well and cover tightly. Simmer 30 minutes or until pork is tender. Cook contents of rice and seasoning packets in chicken stock according to package directions. Pack in lightly oiled loaf pan or ring mold. Add orange marmalade to pork and pan juices. Simmer 5 minutes more. Add parsley. Unmold rice loaf or mold. Surround rice or fill center of ring with pork. Pass gravy separately. Makes 8 servings.

# Ham Loaf With Whipped Horseradish Sauce

*Spread a spicy sauce over a mild-flavored meat loaf.*

1 (6-oz.) pkg. UNCLE BEN'S®
　　Long Grain & Wild Rice
2-1/2 cups water
1 tablespoon butter or margarine
1-1/2 lbs. ground ham

1-1/2 lbs. ground pork
2 eggs, beaten slightly
1/2 (10-3/4-oz.) can condensed
　　tomato soup
Creamy Horseradish Sauce, see below

*Creamy Horseradish Sauce:*
1 cup whipping cream
1/4 cup prepared horseradish

1/4 cup prepared mustard
1 teaspoon sugar

Preheat oven to 350°F (177°C). Butter a shallow baking pan or cookie sheet. Cook contents of rice and seasoning packets with water and butter or margarine according to package directions. Combine ham, pork, eggs, soup and cooked rice. Mix well. Shape into 8-1/2" x 6" x 3" loaf in baking pan. Bake until done, about 1 hour and 15 minutes. Serve with Creamy Horseradish Sauce. Makes 10 to 12 servings.

**Creamy Horseradish Sauce:**
Just before serving, whip cream until very stiff. Fold in horseradish, mustard and sugar. Serve with ham loaf. Makes about 2 cups.

Finely chop drained sauerkraut and corned beef. Mix them together with onion, eggs, cooked rice, cheese, salt and pepper.

Shape 1/4 cup of the corned-beef mixture in a croquette. Make 18 croquettes in all.

# How To Make Reuben Croquettes

Roll each croquette first in fine, dry bread crumbs, then in a mixture of beaten egg and water. Roll again in bread crumbs and set aside for 10 minutes to dry before cooking.

Combine Mustard Sauce ingredients, mix well and serve with croquettes.

# Reuben Croquettes

*The choice is yours—bake or fry 'em. Either way, cooking is quick.*

1/2 cup UNCLE BEN'S® CONVERTED®
  Brand Rice
1-1/3 cups water
1/2 teaspoon salt
1/2 tablespoon butter or margarine
1 (1-lb.) can sauerkraut
1 (12-oz.) can corned beef
1/4 cup chopped onion
2 eggs

1 cup shredded Swiss cheese
1 teaspoon salt
1/4 teaspoon pepper
1 egg
2 tablespoons water
1-1/2 cups fine dry bread crumbs
1 to 2 cups vegetable oil, if frying
Mustard Sauce, see below

*Mustard Sauce:*
1 cup mayonnaise
1/3 cup milk

1/4 cup prepared mustard
4 teaspoons lemon juice

If baking, preheat oven to 450°F (232°C). Cook rice with 1-1/3 cups water, 1/2 teaspoon salt and butter or margarine according to package directions for half the basic recipe. Drain sauerkraut very well, pressing out as much liquid as possible. Chop sauerkraut and corned beef very fine. Add onion, 2 eggs, cooked rice, cheese, 1 teaspoon salt and pepper. Mix well. Shape in 18 croquettes or balls using 1/4 cup of mixture for each. Combine 1 egg and water; beat slightly. Roll each croquette in crumbs, then egg mixture and in crumbs again. Let dry 10 minutes. If frying, cook croquettes in hot shallow oil, 5 to 7 minutes, turning once. If baking, bake 10 minutes; turn and bake 10 minutes longer. Serve croquettes with Mustard Sauce. Makes 6 servings.

**Mustard Sauce:**
Combine and mix mayonnaise, milk, mustard and lemon juice.

# Ham in Orange-Mustard Sauce

*Here's one gourmet dish you can cook in less time than it takes to eat.*

1 (6-oz.) pkg. UNCLE BEN'S®
  Long Grain & Wild Rice
2-1/2 cups water
1 tablespoon butter or margarine
2 tablespoons butter or margarine
1 to 1-1/2 lbs. sliced fully cooked ham

1/3 cup frozen orange-juice concentrate
2 teaspoons sugar
1/2 teaspoon prepared mustard
3 green onions, sliced
1/2 cup chopped pecans

Cook contents of rice and seasoning packets with water and 1 tablespoon butter or margarine according to package directions. In a large skillet melt 2 tablespoons butter or margarine. Add ham and heat. Add orange-juice concentrate, sugar, mustard and green onions. Stir. Spoon sauce over ham slices until heated and slightly thickened. Stir chopped pecans into hot cooked rice. Serve with ham. Makes 6 servings.

# Minted Lamb Supreme

*A domestic dish goes exotic!*

1/4 cup olive or vegetable oil
1 lb. leg of lamb,
    cut in 1/2-in. cubes
1/2 cup chopped onion
1/4 cup lemon juice
1 teaspoon garlic salt
1 teaspoon crushed mint leaves
1/2 teaspoon ginger

2 cups chicken broth
1 (6-1/4-oz.) pkg. UNCLE BEN'S®
    Fast Cooking Long Grain & Wild Rice
1/2 cup chopped dates
1/2 cup coarsely chopped walnuts
Pineapple slices for garnish,
    if desired

Heat oil in a large skillet. Add lamb. Cook until browned and cooked through, but still juicy. Add onion. Cook until tender. Remove meat mixture from skillet. Sprinkle with lemon juice, garlic salt, mint leaves and ginger. Keep warm. Add broth, contents of rice and seasoning packets and dates to skillet. Stir. Bring to a boil and cover. Simmer until all liquid is absorbed, about 5 minutes. Stir in meat mixture and walnuts. Cover and simmer 5 minutes more. Garnish with pineapple slices, if desired. Makes 4 servings.

# Burgundy Short Ribs With Chili Rice

*These highly seasoned ribs are a lot less work than you think.*

2 tablespoons vegetable oil
3 lbs. beef short ribs
3 tablespoons flour
1 cup Burgundy or other dry red wine
1/2 teaspoon salt

1 (1 to 1-3/4-oz.) pkg. chili-
    seasoning mix; reserve 1 tablespoon
1 tablespoon flour
1/2 cup water
Chili Rice, see below

*Chili Rice:*
2 tablespoons butter or margarine
1 cup sliced onion
1 cup UNCLE BEN'S® CONVERTED®
    Brand Rice
2-1/2 cups water

1 teaspoon salt
1 tablespoon chili-seasoning mix
    (reserved from above)
1/2 cup chopped green pepper

Preheat oven to 325°F (163°C). In a large oven-proof skillet, heat oil. Dredge meat in 3 tablespoons flour. Brown well on all sides in hot oil. Sprinkle any remaining flour over meat. Add wine and salt. Reserve 1 tablespoon chili-seasoning mix for the Chili Rice. Add remaining seasoning to short ribs. Cover. Bake until meat is tender, about 2 hours. Transfer short ribs to heated serving dish. Remove excess fat from drippings. Blend 1 tablespoon flour and water. Stir into pan drippings and heat. Serve over short ribs and Chili Rice. Makes 6 servings.

**Chili Rice:**
In a medium saucepan, melt butter or margarine. Add onion and cook until tender. Add rice, water, salt, chili-seasoning mix and green pepper. Stir. Bring to a boil and cover tightly. Simmer 20 minutes. Remove from heat. Let stand until all liquid is absorbed, about 5 minutes.

# Beef Strudel With Burgundy Mushroom Sauce

*Meat-filled pastry—gourmet-style. And so easy!*

1 egg
1 lb. lean ground beef
1 cup UNCLE BEN'S® QUICK™
   Brand Rice
1 (8-oz.) can tomato sauce
1/4 cup chopped green pepper
1/4 cup chopped onion
1 medium carrot, shredded

1 teaspoon salt
1 teaspoon chili powder
1/2 teaspoon seasoned salt
1/4 teaspoon pepper
2 (4.5-oz.) cans refrigerated buttermilk
   biscuits
Burgundy-Mushroom Sauce, see below

*Burgundy Mushroom Sauce:*
2 tablespoons butter or margarine
1/4 lb. fresh mushrooms, sliced
2 tablespoons sliced green onion
1 tablespoon flour

3/4 cup Burgundy or other red wine
1/2 cup water
1 beef-bouillon cube, crushed

Preheat oven to 375°F (191°C). Butter a 15" x 12" baking pan. Beat egg slightly; reserve 1 tablespoon beaten egg for brushing top crust. In a large bowl, combine remaining egg, beef, uncooked rice, tomato sauce, green pepper, onion, carrot, salt, chili powder, seasoned salt and pepper. Mix well. Arrange biscuits side by side in a rectangle on baking pan. Seal biscuits together and pat out with your fingertips to within 1-inch of edge of baking pan. Shape meat mixture lengthwise on dough into a 10" x 3-1/2" loaf. Bring edges of dough up over loaf. Seal edges well. Make 6 to 8 small slashes on top with point of knife. Brush with reserved tablespoon of egg. Bake until crust is well browned, 40 to 45 minutes. Serve Burgundy-Mushroom Sauce over slices of Strudel. Makes 6 to 8 servings.

**Burgundy Mushroom Sauce:**
In a medium saucepan, melt butter or margarine. Add mushrooms and onion. Cook until tender, not brown. Stir in flour. Add Burgundy or other red wine, water and bouillon cube. Cook, uncovered, until slightly thickened. Cover. Simmer to blend flavors, about 20 minutes.

# Broiled Steaks & Wild Rice

*Here's a dish to please hearty appetites.*

1 (6-oz.) pkg. UNCLE BEN'S®
   Long Grain & Wild Rice
2 cups water
1/2 cup dry red wine
1 tablespoon butter or margarine

1 cup dairy sour cream
1 cup sliced fresh mushrooms
3 tablespoons butter or margarine
1 teaspoon Worcestershire sauce
4 strip steaks, 1-in. thick

Preheat broiler. Cook contents of rice and seasoning packets with water, wine and 1 tablespoon butter or margarine according to package directions. Fold in sour cream. Sauté mushrooms in 3 tablespoons butter or margarine 5 minutes. Add Worcestershire sauce; keep warm. About 10 minutes before rice is done, start broiling steaks in preheated broiler. Broil to desired degree of doneness. For medium-rare, broil 1-1/2 to 2 inches from heat source, 5 to 7 minutes per side. Top steaks with mushrooms. Serve with rice. Makes 4 servings.

# Beef & Snow Peas Chinese-Style

*Surprise your family with traditional Chinese fare.*

1 lb. top round beef
1 cup UNCLE BEN'S® CONVERTED®
   Brand Rice
2-1/2 cups water
1 teaspoon salt
1 tablespoon butter or margarine
1 tablespoon cornstarch
2 tablespoons soy sauce
1 tablespoon dry sherry
1/2 teaspoon sugar
1/2 teaspoon salt

1/2 lb. fresh snow-pea pods
Water
3 tablespoons vegetable oil
1 (8-oz.) can water chestnuts, drained
   and sliced
1 tablespoon cornstarch
1 cup water
2 tablespoons chopped green onions
   with tops
2 tablespoons pimiento strips

Chill meat in freezer until slightly firm. Cook rice with 2-1/2 cups water, 1 teaspoon salt and butter or margarine according to package directions. Cut meat diagonally across the grain into very thin slices. Mix 1 tablespoon cornstarch, soy sauce, sherry, sugar and 1/2 teaspoon salt. Pour over meat and mix well. Snap off tips of fresh snow-pea pods and remove strings. Blanch one minute in boiling water, rinse in cold water and drain well. Heat oil in large skillet or wok until very hot. Add snow-pea pods. Cook and stir until pea pods are tender, but still crisp, 4 to 5 minutes. Remove from pan. Drain beef; reserve marinade. Add beef to skillet or wok. Cook and stir until meat is brown, 3 to 4 minutes. Stir in pea pods and water chestnuts. Combine 1 tablespoon cornstarch and water with meat marinade; mix well. Pour over meat mixture. Cook and stir until sauce is thickened and clear. Stir green onion and pimiento into cooked rice and serve with meat mixture. Makes 4 to 6 servings.

**Variation:**
Substitute 1 (7-oz.) package of frozen snow-pea pods, thawed, or 1 (10-oz.) package frozen broccoli spears, thawed, for fresh snow-pea pods.

# Pork Chops Veracruz

*Flavorful pork in a spicy sauce.*

2 tablespoons vegetable oil
6 pork chops, 3/4 to 1-in.-thick
1 tablespoon flour
1 tablespoon brown sugar
1 teaspoon dry mustard
1 teaspoon salt
1 clove garlic, minced
2 medium onions, sliced
1/2 cup dry white wine

1/2 cup water, or as needed
1 medium green pepper, chopped
1 cup UNCLE BEN'S® CONVERTED®
   Brand Rice
2-1/2 cups water
1 teaspoon salt
1 tablespoon butter or margarine
2 to 3 tablespoons coarsely chopped
   pimiento

In a large skillet, heat oil. Add pork chops. Brown well on both sides. Drain off excess fat. Sprinkle with flour, brown sugar, dry mustard, salt and garlic. Add onions and wine. Cover. Cook over low heat until chops are tender, about 1 hour. Add 1/2 cup water, or as needed, and spoon sauce over chops several times. Add green pepper 15 minutes before end of cooking time. Cook rice with 2-1/2 cups water, 1 teaspoon salt and butter or margarine according to package directions. Top pork chops with pimiento and serve with rice. Makes 6 servings.

# Veal Marsala With Risotto

*Tender veal slices in a mushroom-wine sauce.*

1/4 cup flour
Salt and pepper, to taste
1 lb. thin-sliced veal, cut for scallopini
1/4 cup butter or margarine
1 cup thinly sliced mushrooms

1/4 cup hot water
1 beef-bouillon cube
1/4 cup Marsala or white wine
Salt and pepper to taste
Cayenne pepper to taste

*Risotto:*

3 tablespoons butter or margarine
1 medium onion, thinly sliced
1/2 cup red pepper or pimiento,
   slivered

2 cups UNCLE BEN'S® QUICK™
   Brand Rice
1 (10-1/2-oz.) can condensed beef broth
1/4 cup water

Combine flour, salt and pepper. Coat veal slices. In a large skillet, melt butter or margarine. Add veal and brown on both sides. Add mushrooms. Cook until golden. Stir in hot water and bouillon cube, scraping pan. Cook a few minutes until veal is tender. Add wine and heat. Add seasonings to taste. Serve veal in the center or a ring of Risotto. Makes 4 servings.

Risotto:
In a medium saucepan, melt butter or margarine. Add onion and pepper or pimiento and sauté lightly. Add rice, bouillon and water. Bring to a *vigorous* boil and cover. Simmer until all liquid is absorbed, about 5 minutes.

# Lamb Chops With Lemony Wild Rice

*Keep the celery crunchy by tossing it in at the last minute.*

6 lamb-shoulder chops, about
  3/4-in.-thick
2 tablespoons vegetable oil
1 (6-oz.) pkg. UNCLE BEN'S®
  Long Grain & Wild Rice
2-1/2 cups water

1 tablespoon butter or margarine
1 teaspoon salt
1/2 teaspoon garlic salt
1 teaspoon grated lemon peel
1/2 cup sliced celery

Drizzle both sides of chops with oil. Rub contents of rice seasoning packet into surface of chops. Refrigerate 1 hour. Prepare contents of rice packet with water and butter or margarine according to package directions, adding one teaspoon salt. Arrange chops on broiler pan. Broil 4 to 5 inches from heat, about 10 to 15 minutes on each side. Sprinkle cooked chops with garlic salt. Stir lemon peel and celery into cooked rice before serving. Makes 6 servings.

# Lamb Chops & Rice Niçoise

*The flavor-filled marinade is the secret.*

2-1/2 tablespoons vegetable oil
2-1/2 tablespoons olive oil
3 tablespoons vinegar
1 clove garlic, halved
1/2 teaspoon dry mustard
1/2 teaspoon salt
1/8 teaspoon pepper
6 lamb shoulder chops, 3/4-inch thick
1 (1-lb.) can tomatoes
2 teaspoons flour
1 (6-oz.) can pitted ripe olives,
  drained and sliced

2 tablespoons chopped parsley
1 tablespoon dried chopped chives
1/2 teaspoon basil
1/4 teaspoon sugar
4 to 6 anchovy fillets, chopped
3 cups UNCLE BEN'S® QUICK™
  Brand Rice
2-1/3 cups water
1/2 teaspoon salt
1-1/2 tablespoons butter or margarine

In a small bowl, combine vegetable oil, olive oil, vinegar, garlic, dry mustard, salt and pepper. Mix well. Place chops in plastic bag. Pour marinade into bag. Seal bag tightly. Place in shallow dish and refrigerate at least 2 hours, turning bag several times. Remove chops from marinade. Place marinade in a large saucepan. Heat until garlic browns lightly. Remove garlic. Mix tomatoes and flour. Add to marinade in the saucepan. Simmer to thicken, about 10 minutes. Add olives, parsley, chives, basil, sugar and anchovy fillets. Heat. Broil lamb chops 4 to 5 inches from heat until cooked to desired doneness, 10 to 15 minutes, turning once. Cook rice with water, 1/2 teaspoon salt and butter or margarine according to package directions. Serve lamb chops with hot cooked rice. Top with sauce. Makes 6 servings.

# Shish Kebabs With Mint Rice

*Cook outdoors for a tasty patio meal.*

2 lbs. boneless lean lamb (from leg),
   cut in 1/2-in.-chunks
1/3 cup vegetable oil
1/4 cup lemon juice
1/4 cup dry red wine
1 teaspoon salt

1/2 teaspoon rosemary
3 small tomatoes, cut in quarters
2 medium green peppers,
   cut in large chunks
Buttery Mint Rice, see below

*Buttery Mint Rice:*

1/4 cup butter or margarine
1 cup UNCLE BEN'S® CONVERTED®
   Brand Rice
1/4 cup finely chopped onion
Water

1 (13-3/4-oz.) can chicken broth
1 teaspoon salt
1 tablespoon finely chopped parsley
1 tablespoon finely chopped green onion
1 tablespoon finely chopped fresh mint

Place meat in a plastic bag. Combine oil, lemon juice, wine, salt and rosemary. Mix well. Pour over lamb; close bag securely. Marinate in refrigerator at least 2 hours or overnight, turning several times. Drain lamb; reserve marinade. Thread lamb chunks onto 6 skewers. Thread tomato and green pepper alternately onto 6 other skewers. Grill lamb over medium-high heat to the degree of preferred doneness, about 10 to 12 minutes total time, turning once. Brush vegetables with marinade. Grill just until heated, about 3 to 5 minutes. Serve lamb with vegetable kebabs with Buttery Mint Rice. Makes 6 servings.

**Buttery Mint Rice:**

In a large saucepan, melt butter or margarine. Add rice and onion. Cook until rice is golden brown, stirring occasionally. Add water to chicken broth to make 2-1/2 cups liquid. Add liquid and 1 teaspoon salt to rice. Heat to boiling and cover. Simmer 20 minutes. Remove from heat. Let stand, covered, until all liquid is absorbed, about 5 minutes. Stir in parsley, green onion and mint.

# Baked Pork Chops & Brown Rice

*A healthful blend of meat, vegetables and natural rice.*

1 cup UNCLE BEN'S®
  Brown Rice
1-1/2 teaspoons salt
1/2 teaspoon rosemary
1 tablespoon butter or margarine
6 pork chops, cut 3/4-in. thick
  (about 2-1/2 lbs.)

1 tablespoon butter or margarine
2 cups thinly sliced carrots
1/2 cup chopped onion
1 small clove garlic, minced
2-1/2 cups boiling water
1/2 teaspoon salt

Preheat oven to 350°F (177°C). Place rice, 1-1/2 teaspoons salt and rosemary in a shallow 2-quart casserole. In a large skillet, melt 1 tablespoon butter or margarine. Brown chops on both sides. Remove from skillet; set aside. Melt 1 tablespoon butter or margarine in skillet. Add carrots, onion and garlic. Cook until onion is tender. Add to rice in casserole. Stir in boiling water. Top with pork chops. Sprinkle with 1/2 teaspoon salt. Cover tightly. Bake until chops and rice are tender, about 1 hour. Uncover. Return to oven until all water is absorbed, 5 to 10 minutes. Makes 6 servings.

# Pork-Pear Casserole

*Fruit, pork and spices in a subtle blend.*

2 tablespoons butter or margarine
6 pork chops, cut 1-in.-thick
1 teaspoon salt
1/4 teaspoon pepper
2 tablespoons butter or margarine
1 (6-oz.) pkg. UNCLE BEN'S®
  Long Grain & Wild Rice

1/2 cup chopped onion
1/4 cup chopped celery
2-1/4 cups boiling water
1-1/2 cups chopped, unpeeled fresh pears
1/4 cup seedless raisins
1/8 teaspoon ground coriander
1/8 teaspoon cardamom

In a large skillet melt 2 tablespoons butter or margarine. Add chops and brown on both sides. Sprinkle salt and pepper over chops; set aside. Melt 2 tablespoons butter or margarine in a Dutch oven or large skillet. Add contents of rice packet, onion and celery. Cook until onion is tender and rice lightly browned, about 5 minutes. Dissolve contents of seasoning packet in boiling water. Stir into rice mixture. Fold in pears, raisins, coriander and cardamom. Top with pork chops and cover. Simmer over low to moderate heat until chops are tender, about 1 hour. Makes 6 servings.

# Pork Chops California-Style

*Johnny Appleseed's favorite.*

1 tablespoon vegetable shortening
6 rib pork chops (about 2 lbs.)
1 teaspoon salt
1 cup UNCLE BEN'S® CONVERTED®
   Brand Rice
3/4 cup seedless raisins
3/4 cup sliced onion

1/4 cup brown sugar, firmly packed
1/4 teaspoon ground nutmeg
1 teaspoon salt
1-1/2 cups water
1 cup apple juice
1 firm cooking apple

Preheat oven to 350°F (177°C). In a large skillet, melt shortening. Add chops and brown well on both sides. Season chops with 1 teaspoon salt. In a shallow 2-quart casserole, combine rice, raisins, onion, brown sugar, nutmeg and 1 teaspoon salt. Mix well. Heat water and apple juice just to boiling. Pour over rice mixture. Top with chops. Core apple and cut into 12 wedges. Arrange 2 wedges on each chop. Cover with aluminum foil, crimping it securely to edge of casserole. Bake until chops are fork-tender, about 1 hour. Uncover for last 5 minutes of cooking time. Makes 6 servings.

# Pork Chops Rio Grande

*Tender chops with vegetable-topped rice mounds.*

1 cup UNCLE BEN'S® CONVERTED®
   Brand Rice
2-1/2 cups water
1 teaspoon salt
1 tablespoon butter or margarine
4 lean pork chops
1/4 cup diced onion

1/3 cup diced celery
2 tablespoons diced green pepper
1-1/2 cups canned tomatoes
1-1/2 teaspoons salt
1/4 teaspoon pepper
2 tablespoons minced parsley

Preheat oven to 350°F (177°C). Cook rice with water and 1 tablespoon butter or margarine according to package directions. Keep warm. Brown chops in a large skillet. Remove chops. Add onion, celery and green pepper to drippings. Sauté until tender. Add tomatoes, salt and pepper. Simmer 10 minutes. Place chops in baking dish and sprinkle with salt and pepper. Top each with mound of 1/2 cup cooked rice. Pour sauce over all and sprinkle with parsley. Cover. Bake for approximately 1 hour. Just before serving, spoon sauce over chops. Makes 4 servings.

# How To Make
# Pork Chops Rio Grande

Brown chops, remove from skillet and place in a baking dish.

Using a half-cup measure, top each chop with a mound of cooked rice.

Make sauce with the pork drippings. Pour sauce over the rice mounds and chops. Sprinkle with parsley and bake.

# Surprise Pie

*If you like quiche, try this new recipe.*

1-1/3 cups UNCLE BEN'S® QUICK™
  Brand Rice
1 cup water
1-1/2 teaspoons butter or margarine
1/4 teaspoon salt
1 (10-in.) unbaked pastry shell
  with 2-in.-high fluted edge
3 eggs, slightly beaten
1/2 teaspoon salt

1/2 teaspoon Worcestershire sauce
Dash of pepper
1-1/2 cups half and half, scalded
1/2 lb. chunk beef bologna, diced
1/4 lb. Swiss cheese, shredded
1 cup cooked chopped broccoli
1 tablespoon butter or margarine
1/4 cup slivered almonds

Preheat oven to 450°F (232°C). Cook rice with water, 1-1/2 teaspoons butter or margarine and 1/4 teaspoon salt according to package directions. Prick pastry crust. Bake 5 minutes. Do not turn oven off. In a large bowl, combine eggs, salt, Worcestershire sauce and pepper. Add half and half, beating constantly. Stir in bologna, cheese, broccoli and 1 cup cooked rice. Pour into crust. Bake at 450°F (232°C) 10 minutes. Reduce heat to 300°F (149°C) and continue baking until filling is set, 30 to 35 minutes. Let stand 10 minutes. Melt 1 tablespoon butter or margarine. Add remaining rice and almonds. Heat and stir until hot, and almonds are lightly toasted. Sprinkle evenly over top of pie. Cut in wedges. Makes 6 to 8 servings.


# Bengal Beef

*Calm your wanderlust with this adventure in taste.*

2 tablespoons vegetable oil
1-1/2 lbs. beef round or chuck, cut
  in 1-in.-cubes
4 medium onions, sliced
1 clove garlic, minced
1 tablespoon curry powder
1 tablespoon flour
1-1/2 teaspoons salt
1 beef-bouillon cube, crumbled

1-1/2 cups water
1/4 cup vinegar
1/2 cup seedless raisins
1 cup UNCLE BEN'S® CONVERTED®
  Brand Rice
2-1/2 cups water
1 teaspoon salt
1 tablespoon butter or margarine
1 (8-oz.) carton plain yogurt, if desired

In a large skillet, heat oil. Add beef. Brown well on all sides. Remove from skillet. Add onions and garlic. Cook until tender, but not brown. Add curry powder, Stir and cook 2 to 3 minutes, being careful curry powder does not burn. Stir in flour and 1-1/2 teaspoons salt. Add bouillon cube, water, vinegar and raisins. Stir and cover. Cook over low heat until meat is tender, 2 to 2-1/2 hours, stirring several times. Cook rice with water, 1 teaspoon salt and butter or margarine according to package directions. Serve with beef. Top with yogurt, if desired. Makes 6 servings.

# Short Ribs Italian-Style

*Pungent gravy brimming with vegetables makes this a hearty one-dish meal.*

2 tablespoons olive oil
8 short ribs (about 3 lbs.)
2 onions, sliced
2 cloves garlic, minced
2 ribs celery, sliced
3 carrots, sliced
1/2 cup dry red wine
1/2 cup water
1 teaspoon oregano
1/2 teaspoon rosemary

1 teaspoon salt
1 (6-oz.) can tomato paste
1 (10-1/2-oz.) can condensed beef bouillon
1 soup-can water
1 tablespoon butter or margarine
1/2 teaspoon salt
1 cup UNCLE BEN'S® CONVERTED®
   Brand Rice
1/4 cup chopped parsley

In a Dutch oven or large cast iron skillet, heat oil. Add short ribs. Brown on all sides. Add onions, garlic, celery and carrots. Cook 2 minutes, stirring constantly. Add wine, water, oregano, rosemary, 1 teaspoon salt and tomato paste. Cover. Simmer over low heat, turning occasionally, until tender, about 1-1/2 hours. Bring bouillon, soup-can water, butter or margarine and 1/2 teaspoon salt to a boil. Add rice. Cover tightly and simmer 20 minutes. Remove from heat. Let stand, covered, until all liquid is absorbed, about 5 minutes. Stir in parsley. Serve short ribs on rice. Pass gravy separately to spoon over meat and rice. Makes 4 servings.

# Lamb Curry Calcutta

*If you enjoy adventurous cooking, try this thick, rich curry.*

2 tablespoons vegetable oil
2 lbs. boneless lamb, cut in
   1-1/2-in.-cubes
3 medium onions, chopped
2 cooking apples, chopped
2 cloves garlic, minced
1 tablespoon curry powder
1/8 teaspoon cayenne pepper
2 tablespoons flour

2 teaspoons salt
1 (13-3/4-oz.) can beef broth
1/2 cup half and half
1 cup UNCLE BEN'S® CONVERTED®
   Brand Rice
2-1/2 cups water
1 teaspoon salt
1 tablespoon butter or margarine
1/2 cup raisins

In a large skillet, heat oil. Add meat cubes and brown on all sides. Add onions, apples and garlic. Cook until onion is tender, but not brown, stirring frequently. Add curry powder, cayenne pepper, flour and salt, stirring well to coat meat evenly. Add beef broth and stir. Heat until sauce bubbles. Stir in half and half. Cover. Cook over low heat until meat is tender, about 1-1/2 to 2 hours, stirring occasionally. During last 1/2 hour cook rice with water, 1 teaspoon salt and butter or margarine according to package directions. Stir raisins into rice before serving with lamb. Makes 6 servings.

**Variation:**
Substitute beef cubes for lamb cubes.

# Baked Stroganoff Meatballs

*Here's royal treatment for ground beef!*

1-1/2 lbs. lean ground beef
1 small onion, finely chopped
1/4 cup grated Parmesan cheese
1/3 cup milk
1 egg, beaten
1 teaspoon salt
1 teaspoon Worcestershire sauce
Dash pepper
1 (10-3/4-oz.) can cream-of-mushroom soup

1 beef-bouillon cube, crumbled
1 (6-oz.) pkg. UNCLE BEN'S®
  Long Grain & Wild Rice
1 (4-oz.) can mushroom stems and pieces
1 tablespoon butter or margarine
2-1/4 cups boiling water
1/2 cup dairy sour cream
1 (2-oz.) jar sliced pimiento, drained

Preheat oven to 400°F (205°C). In a large bowl, combine beef, onion, Parmesan cheese, milk, egg, salt, Worcestershire sauce and pepper. Mix well. Shape into 18 meatballs. Place in a 2-quart baking dish. Bake, uncovered, for 15 minutes. Drain off fat. Stir in soup and bouillon cube. Reduce oven temperature to 350°F (177°C) and bake, uncovered, for 45 minutes. Place contents of rice and seasoning packets, mushrooms and butter or margarine in a 1-quart casserole. Add boiling water, stir and cover. Bake in oven beside baking dish with meat balls, about 40 minutes, or until all liquid is absorbed. Remove meatballs from oven; stir in sour cream. Return to oven and heat 5 minutes. Stir pimiento into rice. Serve with meatballs. Makes 6 servings.

# Cantonese-Style Beef & Green Beans

*Quick-cooking meat and vegetables, Chinese style, with natural juices.*

1 cup UNCLE BEN'S® CONVERTED®
  Brand Rice
2-1/2 cups water
1 teaspoon salt
1 tablespoon butter or margarine
1 lb. top beef round, partially frozen
1 tablespoon cornstarch
2 tablespoons soy sauce
1 teaspoon sugar

1 teaspoon garlic salt
2 tablespoons vegetable oil
1 (9-oz.) pkg. frozen cut green beans, thawed
1 cup sliced celery
6 green onions, cut in 1-in. lengths
1 (2-oz.) jar sliced pimiento
1 tablespoon cornstarch
1 cup water

Cook rice with 2-1/2 cups water, salt and butter or margarine according to package directions. Slice meat in very thin strips. In a large bowl, combine 1 tablespoon cornstarch, soy sauce, sugar and garlic salt. Add meat; mix well. Heat oil in a large skillet. Add meat and cornstarch mixture. Cook and stir over high heat until meat is browned, about 3 to 4 minutes. Add green beans. Stir and cook 5 minutes. Add celery, green onions and pimiento; stir. Combine 1 tablespoon cornstarch and 1 cup water. Pour over vegetables. Cook until sauce is thickened. Serve over rice. Makes 6 servings.

**Variation:**
Substitute peas or broccoli flowerets for green beans.

# Poultry

Rice is a seasoned world traveler, blending well with sauces, curries, cheeses, fruits and vegetables from the far corners of the world. People in nearly every country prepare special dishes from rice and chicken. UNCLE BEN'S® has gathered an interesting variety of these recipes for you to try. From south of the border comes Mexican Fruited Chicken. Chicken Oriental brings you flavors from China. West Indian Chicken Curry is especially for those with exotic tastes. You'll enjoy these recipes combining flavors from other lands.

*Taste Travel to Mexico*
* Mexican Fruited Chicken
  Avocado & Red-Onion Salad
  Bananas Flambé Over Ice Cream

*Salute to Italy Night*
* Chicken Mozzarella Bake
  Buttered Zucchini Sticks
  Tossed Green Salad,
  Zesty Dressing
  Italian Bread
  Lemon Ice

*A Touch of The Orient*
* Chicken Oriental
  Snow Peas Sauté
  Orange Sherbet
  Fortune Cookies

*Day After the Holiday*
* Turkey-Almond Custard
  Peas and Mushrooms
  Apple-Walnut Salad
  Chocolate Pudding Cake

*Let's Entertain California Style*
* Napa Valley Chicken
  Ceasar Salad
  Sourdough Bread
  Cheese Tray & Fruit

*Informal Party*
* Tangerine Chicken
  Buttered Frenched Green Beans
    and Mushrooms
  Sliced Tomatoes,
  Olive Oil Dressing
  Vanilla Ice Cream Crepes,
  Chocolate Sauce

*These recipes are in this section.*

# Chicken & Ham With Wild Rice

*A bit of old southern cooking.*

1 (6-oz.) pkg. UNCLE BEN'S®
   Long Grain & Wild Rice
2-1/2 cups water
1 tablespoon butter or margarine
2 tablespoons butter or margarine
1 cup sliced fresh mushrooms

2 cups diced cooked chicken
1 cup diced cooked ham
1 (4-oz.) jar pimiento, drained and chopped
1/2 cup coarsely chopped salted peanuts
1 tablespoon chopped parsley

Cook contents of rice and seasoning packets with water and 1 tablespoon butter or margarine according to package directions. In a large skillet, melt 2 tablespoons butter or margarine. Add mushrooms. Cook until tender, not brown. Add chicken and ham. Heat, stirring frequently. Add rice and pimiento. Stir and heat thoroughly. Sprinkle with peanuts and parsley. Makes 6 servings.

# Sweet & Pungent Chicken & Rice

*Spicy marinade and sauce make this a special dish.*

2-1/2 to 3 lbs. chicken pieces
3/4 cup soy sauce
1/3 cup vegetable oil
1/3 cup sherry
1 teaspoon ground ginger
1 large clove garlic, crushed

2 cups UNCLE BEN'S® QUICK™
   Brand Rice
1-1/2 cups chicken stock
1/4 teaspoon salt
1/2 cup sliced green-onion tops
2 tablespoons butter or margarine
Sherry Sauce, see below

*Sherry Sauce:*
1/4 cup reserved marinade
1/4 cup sherry
1/4 cup apricot or pineapple preserves

1 tablespoon cornstarch
1 tablespoon sugar
1/2 cup water

Place chicken in a shallow casserole. In a small bowl, mix soy sauce, vegetable oil, sherry, ginger and garlic. Pour over chicken. Cover and refrigerate at least 4 hours or overnight. Lightly butter a shallow baking pan. About an hour before serving preheat oven to 400°F (205°C). Drain chicken and reserve 1/4 cup marinade for the sauce. Use the remaining marinade for basting. Place chicken skin side down in buttered baking pan. Bake for 30 minutes, brushing with marinade every 10 minutes. Turn chicken; brush with marinade. Bake 20 minutes longer, basting again after 10 minutes. About 10 minutes before chicken is done, combine rice, chicken stock and salt in a medium saucepan. Bring to a *vigorous* boil and cover. Simmer until all water is absorbed, about 5 minutes, or until rice is tender. Just before serving, stir in sliced green-onion tops and butter or margarine. Makes 4 servings.

## Sherry Sauce:

In a small saucepan, heat reserved marinade with sherry and preserves. Combine cornstarch and sugar, stir in water to make a thin paste. Stir into hot marinade mixture. Cook, stirring, until sauce thickens and boils. Serve with chicken and rice. Makes about 2 cups.

# Napa Valley Chicken

*Whip up a popular meal with little effort.*

1 clove garlic, sliced
2 tablespoons olive oil
2 tablespoons butter or margarine
3 lbs. chicken pieces
1 cup UNCLE BEN'S® CONVERTED®
   Brand Rice
1 cup sliced fresh mushrooms

1 (3-3/4-oz.) can pitted black olives, drained
2 teaspoons salt
1/4 teaspoon thyme
1 bay leaf
1 (13-3/4-oz.) can chicken broth
1 (8-1/4-oz.) can tomatoes
1/2 cup dry sherry

Preheat oven to 350°F (177°C). In a large skillet with heatproof handle, lightly brown garlic in oil. Remove garlic. Add butter or margarine. Add chicken pieces. Brown well on all sides. Add rice, mushrooms, olives, salt, thyme and bay leaf. Add chicken broth, tomatoes and sherry, making certain rice is covered with liquid. Cover. Bake until chicken is tender, 40 to 45 minutes. Remove bay leaf. Makes 6 servings.


# Plum-Glazed Duckling, Apricot Rice

*A gourmet's delight.*

1 (5-lb.) duckling, fresh or frozen, quartered
1/2 teaspoon salt
1 (12-oz.) jar plum preserves
1/4 cup light corn syrup
1/4 cup orange juice

1 teaspoon grated orange peel
1/4 teaspoon ground ginger
1/4 cup toasted slivered almonds
Apricot Rice, see below

*Apricot Rice:*
1 (1-lb.) can apricot halves
Water
1 tablespoon butter or margarine

1 (6-oz.) pkg. UNCLE BEN'S®
   Long Grain & Wild Rice
1/2 teaspoon grated orange peel

Thaw duckling, if frozen. Preheat oven to 325°F (163°C). Wash, drain and dry duckling quarters. Sprinkle salt evenly over all sides. Place on rack in shallow roasting pan, skin side up. Bake until drumstick meat is tender, about 2 hours, turning several times, ending with skin side up. While duckling is baking, combine plum preserves, corn syrup, orange juice, orange peel and ginger. Bring to a boil. Boil 1 minute. Spoon glaze over duckling several times during last 30 minutes of baking. Sprinkle almonds over duckling. Serve duck with Apricot Rice and any remaining glaze. Makes 4 to 6 servings.

**Apricot Rice:**
Drain apricot halves; reserve syrup. Add water to syrup to make 2-1/2 cups liquid. In a large saucepan combine liquid and butter or margarine. Bring to a boil. Stir in contents of rice and seasoning packets. Stir and cover. Simmer 25 minutes or until liquid is absorbed. Remove from heat. Stir in apricot halves and orange peel.

# Chicken Casserole Véronique

*Green grapes add a French touch.*

1 (6-oz.) pkg. UNCLE BEN'S®
  Long Grain & Wild Rice
1 cup boiling water
2 tablespoons butter or margarine
1 cup chopped celery
1/2 cup chopped green onion
2 (10-1/2-oz.) cans condensed
  cream-of-mushroom soup

1 (4-oz.) can mushroom pieces, undrained
1/3 cup chopped pimiento
1 (8-oz.) can water chestnuts, drained
  and sliced
3 cups cubed cooked chicken
Sauce Véronique, see below

*Sauce Véronique:*

2 tablespoons butter or margarine
2 tablespoons flour
1/2 teaspoon monosodium glutamate,
  if desired
1/2 teaspoon salt

1-1/2 cups chicken broth
2 tablespoons lemon juice
2 tablespoons sugar
1 cup halved seedless green grapes

Preheat oven to 350°F (177°C). Pour contents of rice and seasoning packets over bottom of 12" x 8" baking dish. Stir in boiling water. In a small skillet, melt butter or margarine. Add celery. Cook until tender, not brown. Stir celery, onion, soup, mushrooms and pimiento into rice. Cover with aluminum foil, crimping it tightly to edges of dish. Bake 45 minutes. Remove from oven; remove foil. Fold in water chestnuts and chicken. Return to oven to heat, about 15 minutes. Spoon Sauce Véronique over each individual serving. Makes 6 to 8 servings.

Sauce Véronique:

In a large saucepan, melt butter or margarine. Stir in flour, monosodium glutamate, if desired, and salt. Add chicken broth. Cook until thickened, stirring constantly. Stir in remaining ingredients.

# Chicken-Mozzarella Bake

*Enjoy extra flavor and free time by using onion-soup mix.*

3 tablespoons vegetable oil
4 chicken thighs
4 chicken drumsticks
1 (1-lb.) can stewed tomatoes
1 cup dry white wine
Water

1 cup UNCLE BEN'S® CONVERTED®
  Brand Rice
1 envelope dry onion-soup mix
1/4 teaspoon pepper
2 cups shredded mozzarella cheese

Preheat oven to 325°F (163°C). In a 2-quart oven-proof skillet, heat oil. Add chicken thighs and drumsticks. Fry until brown, turning to brown evenly on all sides. Remove from skillet and keep warm. Drain off excess fat. Drain tomatoes; reserve juice. Combine juice and wine. Add water to make 2-1/2 cups liquid. Pour liquid into skillet. Add tomatoes, rice, onion-soup mix and pepper. Stir. Bring to a boil. Place chicken pieces on top and cover. Bake 45 minutes. Uncover. Sprinkle cheese over top. Return to oven. Bake, uncovered, until chicken is tender and cheese is melted, about 15 minutes. Makes 4 servings.

# Chicken Oriental

*Chinese black mushrooms complete the authenticity of this stir-fry dish.*

5 dried black mushrooms
Hot water
5-1/2 cups water
2 cups UNCLE BEN'S® CONVERTED®
  Brand Rice
2 teaspoons salt
2 teaspoons cornstarch
1 teaspoon sugar
1 teaspoon salt
3 tablespoons soy sauce

2 tablespoons water
2 tablespoons rice wine or dry sherry
1/2 teaspoon monosodium glutamate,
  if desired
3 whole chicken breasts, skinned and
  boned
2 tablespoons vegetable oil
2 tablespoons chopped preserved ginger
1 (4-oz.) can sliced bamboo shoots

Soak mushrooms in hot water for 30 minutes. In a large saucepan, bring 5-1/2 cups of water to a boil. Add rice and salt. Stir gently. Cover tightly. Cook over low heat for 15 minutes. In a small bowl, combine cornstarch, sugar, salt, soy sauce, 2 tablespoons water, rice wine or sherry and monosodium glutamate, if desired, stirring well. Cut chicken into 1-inch pieces and place in a large bowl. Pour 1/3 of the marinade over chicken, mixing well. Drain and chop mushrooms. In a wok or large skillet, heat oil. Quickly stir in ginger. Add chicken pieces and sauté for 1 minute. Add mushroom pieces and bamboo shoots, stir together. Pour remaining marinade over mixture. Stir quickly to mix. Remove skillet from heat. Do not overcook. Put chicken mixture on top of partially cooked rice. Cover, and continue cooking over very low heat 10 to 15 minutes. Makes 8 to 10 servings.

# West Indian Chicken Curry

*A tempting dinner treat from the Caribbean.*

2 tablespoons vegetable oil
3 lbs. chicken pieces
1 teaspoon salt
1 teaspoon curry powder
1/2 teaspoon ground ginger

1 clove garlic, minced
1/2 cup seedless raisins
1 cup orange juice
1 tablespoon cornstarch
1 tablespoon sugar

*Orange Rice:*
1 cup UNCLE BEN'S® CONVERTED®
   Brand Rice
2-1/2 cups water
1 teaspoon salt

1 tablespoon butter or margarine
1/2 cup chopped cashews
2 teaspoons grated orange peel
Chutney, if desired

In a large skillet, heat oil. Add chicken pieces and brown. Drain off fat. Sprinkle chicken with salt, curry powder, ginger, garlic and raisins. In a small bowl, combine orange juice, cornstarch and sugar. Mix until free of lumps. Pour over chicken and cover. Cook over low heat, turning several times, until chicken is tender, about 45 minutes. Remove chicken to serving platter. Simmer sauce to thicken, if desired. Spoon over chicken. Makes 6 servings.

Orange Rice:
Cook rice with water, salt and butter or margarine according to package directions. Stir in cashews and orange peel. Serve with chicken. Serve with chutney, if desired.

# Brandied Chicken Breasts

*This superb creamy sauce raises chicken above the ordinary.*

3 tablespoons butter or margarine
2 or 3 large chicken breasts, split
1 teaspoon salt
1/4 cup brandy
1 (6-oz.) pkg. UNCLE BEN'S®
   Long Grain & Wild Rice

2-1/2 cups water
1 tablespoon butter or margarine
1/2 cup heavy cream
2 egg yolks, beaten
1/4 cup chopped parsley
Salt to taste

In a large skillet, melt 3 tablespoons butter or margarine. Add chicken. Brown on all sides. Add salt and brandy. Cover. Cook over low heat until chicken is tender, 30 to 45 minutes. About 1/2 hour before chicken is done, cook contents of rice and seasoning packets with water and 1 tablespoon butter or margarine according to package directions. Remove chicken from skillet and keep warm. To liquid in pan add cream and heat. Stir a little of the hot mixture into beaten egg yolks and mix well. Pour egg mixture into pan. Cook, stirring constantly, until smooth and thickened. *Do not boil.* Add parsley and salt to taste. Add chicken. Serve with rice. Pass extra sauce separately. Makes 4 to 6 servings.

**West Indian Chicken Curry**

# Tangerine Chicken

*Simmer tender chicken in rosemary-wine seasoning and top with avocados and apricots.*

2/3 cup dry white vermouth
3 tablespoons water
2 tablespoons rosemary, crushed
3/4 cup flour
1-1/2 teaspoons salt
1/2 teaspoon ground ginger
1/4 teaspoon pepper
1 (6-oz.) can frozen tangerine- or orange-juice
   concentrate, thawed

Water
4 lbs. chicken pieces
3 tablespoons butter or margarine
3 tablespoons vegetable oil
Tangerine Rice, see below
2 medium avocados, peeled and sliced lengthwise
1 (29-oz.) can apricot halves, drained

*Tangerine Rice:*

1-1/2 cups UNCLE BEN'S® CONVERTED®
   Brand Rice
3-1/3 cups water
1-1/2 teaspoons salt
1-1/2 tablespoons butter or margarine
6 tablespoons tangerine- or orange-juice
   concentrate (reserved from above)

1 tablespoon dry white vermouth
1 teaspoon salt
1/4 teaspoon pepper
Dash of cinnamon
1 (10-oz.) pkg. frozen peas, partially thawed
1 (4-oz.) jar pimiento, drained and sliced
1/4 cup chopped green onions with tops

In small bowl, combine vermouth, water and rosemary. Let stand, covered, 1 hour. In a medium bowl, mix flour, salt, ginger and pepper. Reserve 6 tablespoons tangerine- or orange-juice concentrate for Tangerine Rice. Add water to remaining concentrate to make 1/2 cup liquid. Dip chicken pieces in liquid. Drain and coat lightly with seasoned flour. In a large skillet, heat butter or margarine and oil. Add chicken pieces. Brown well, turning to brown evenly. Add vermouth-rosemary mixture. Cover loosely. Simmer until liquid evaporates, about 35 minutes. Preheat oven to 375°F (190°C). Spread Tangerine Rice over bottom of 13-1/2" x 8-1/2" baking dish. Arrange chicken pieces on rice in a single layer. Cover with aluminum foil, crimping it tightly to edges of dish. Bake 20 minutes. Uncover. Continue baking until thoroughly heated, about 10 minutes. Garnish with avodaco slices and apricot halves. Makes 6 to 8 servings.

Tangerine Rice:
Cook rice with water, 1-1/2 teaspoons salt and 1-1/2 tablespoons butter or margarine according to package directions. In a small bowl, combine 6 tablespoons tangerine- or orange-juice concentrate, melted butter or margarine, vermouth, 1 teaspoon salt, pepper and cinnamon. Mix well. Pour over rice. Toss lightly. Stir in peas, pimiento and green onions.

# Gourmet Stuffed Chicken Breasts

*Succulent chicken over gently flavored stuffing mounds.*

1 tablespoon butter or margarine
1 (6-oz.) pkg. UNCLE BEN'S®
   Long Grain & Wild Rice
2 tablespoons chopped onion
1-1/2 cups water

1 cup dry sherry
3/4 cup toasted chopped almonds
6 whole chicken breasts, skinned and boned
1/2 teaspoon salt
6 slices bacon, cut in half

Preheat oven to 350°F (177°C). In a large saucepan melt butter or margarine. Add contents of rice packet and onion. Cook until lightly browned, stirring constantly. Stir in water, sherry and contents of seasoning packet. Bring to a boil and cover. Simmer until all liquid is absorbed, about 25 minutes. Stir in almonds. Divide rice mixture into 6 equal mounds (a rounded 1/2 cup each) in a 12" x 8" baking dish. Cover each mound with a chicken breast. Sprinkle with salt. Arrange 2 pieces of bacon over each chicken breast. Cover with aluminum foil, crimping it tightly to edges of dish. Bake 45 minutes. Remove foil and continue baking until chicken is tender, about 30 minutes. Makes 6 servings.

# Apricot Chicken au Vin

*Herbed chicken in apricot-wine sauce. Mmmm!*

1 (1-lb.) can apricot halves
1 (6-oz.) pkg. UNCLE BEN'S®
   Long Grain & Wild Rice
2-1/2 cups water
1 tablespoon butter or margarine
2 tablespoons butter or margarine
3 lbs. chicken pieces

1 cup chopped celery
1 (8-oz.) can water chestnuts, drained and sliced
1/2 teaspoon rosemary
1/4 teaspoon salt
Apricot Glaze, see below
2 tablespoons chopped parsley

*Apricot Glaze:*

4 teaspoons cornstarch
1/4 teaspoon salt

Apricot syrup reserved from can of apricots
1/2 cup dry white wine

Preheat oven to 375°F (191°C). Drain apricots; reserve syrup for glaze. Cook contents of rice and seasoning packets with water and 1 tablespoon butter or margarine according to package directions. In a large skillet, melt 2 tablespoons butter or margarine. Add chicken and brown, turn to brown evenly. Remove chicken pieces from pan; set aside. Add celery, water chestnuts, rosemary and salt to pan drippings. Cook until celery is tender, not brown. Stir in cooked rice. Turn into a 13-1/2" x 8-1/2" baking dish. Arrange chicken pieces over top. Cover with aluminum foil, crimping it tightly to edges of dish. Bake until chicken is tender, about 30 minutes. Uncover chicken; spoon 1/2 of Apricot Glaze over chicken. Return to oven 10 minutes. Garnish with apricot halves. Pour remaining Apricot Glaze over apricots and chicken. Return to oven to heat, about 5 minutes. Sprinkle with parsley. Makes 6 servings.

Apricot Glaze:
Combine cornstarch, salt, reserved apricot syrup and wine. Stir until free of lumps. Cook until thickened, stirring constantly. Makes about 1-1/2 cups.

# Turkey-Almond Custard

*A main-dish custard full of surprises.*

1 (6-oz.) pkg. UNCLE BEN'S®
  Long Grain & Wild Rice
2-1/2 cups water
1 tablespoon butter or margarine
1 (10-1/2-oz.) can chicken gravy
1/2 cup half and half
4 eggs, beaten

1 teaspoon dry mustard
1 teaspoon salt
1/2 teaspoon poultry seasoning
2 cups diced cooked turkey
1/3 cup sliced green onion
1/2 cup slivered almonds

Preheat oven to 350°F (177°C). Butter a shallow 2-quart casserole. Cook contents of rice and seasoning packets with water and butter or margarine according to package directions; keep warm. Combine gravy, half and half, eggs, dry mustard, salt and poultry seasoning. Mix well. Stir in cooked rice, turkey, onion and half of the almonds. Pour into buttered casserole. Bake until custard is set, 30 to 35 minutes. Sprinkle remaining almonds over top after 15 minutes baking. Let stand 10 minutes before cutting. Makes 8 servings.

# Calypso Chicken

*Fruited curry—a West Indian favorite.*

1 (3-1/2-oz.) can flaked coconut
2 cups boiling water
Water
2 tablespoons butter or margarine
3 large chicken breasts, cut in half
1 medium onion, chopped
1 clove garlic, minced
1 tablespoon brown sugar
1 teaspoon salt
1-1/2 to 2 teaspoons curry powder

1/8 teaspoon pepper
1 bay leaf
1 cup UNCLE BEN'S® CONVERTED®
  Brand Rice
1 teaspoon salt
1 ripe avocado, sliced
2 cups fresh pineapple chunks, chilled
1 medium banana, chopped
Chopped cantaloupe for garnish

Place coconut in a medium saucepan. Pour boiling water over coconut. Cover and let stand 15 to 20 minutes. Drain coconut well; reserve liquid. Press as much liquid out of the coconut as possible. Add water to coconut liquid to make 2-1/2 cups. In a large skillet, heat butter or margarine. Add chicken breasts and brown well. Add onion and garlic. Combine brown sugar, 1 teaspoon salt, curry powder and pepper. Sprinkle over chicken. Add bay leaf and 1/2 cup coconut liquid. Cover. Cook over low heat for 20 minutes. Remove chicken. Add rice, remaining coconut liquid and 1 teaspoon salt; stir. Bring to a boil. Arrange chicken breasts on rice and cover. Cook over low heat until most of the liquid is absorbed and chicken is tender, about 20 minutes. Remove from heat. Let stand, covered, until liquid is absorbed, 5 to 10 minutes. Remove bay leaf. Garnish with avocado slices and chopped cantaloupe. Serve with chilled pineapple chunks and chopped banana. Makes 6 servings.

**Calypso Chicken**

# Cornish Hens With Wild Rice

*Delicious served with a light fruit salad.*

1 (6-oz.) pkg. UNCLE BEN'S®
  Long Grain & Wild Rice
2 cups chicken broth
1 tablespoon butter or margarine
2 tablespoons butter or margarine
2 cups thinly sliced fresh mushrooms
1 cup finely diced celery

2/3 cup finely chopped green onions with tops
1/2 cup dairy sour cream
4 (1-lb.) rock Cornish game hens, thawed,
  rinsed and dried
2 tablespoons butter or margarine
1/2 teaspoon salt

Preheat oven to 350°F (177°C). Cook contents of rice and seasoning packets with chicken broth and 1 tablespoon butter or margarine according to package directions. In a medium skillet, melt 2 tablespoons butter or margarine over low heat. Add mushrooms, celery and onions. Cook until tender, not brown. Add cooked rice and sour cream; mix well. Stuff Cornish hens with rice-stuffing mixture, using about 1/2 cup in each. Close opening with skewers. Arrange hens on rack in a shallow baking pan. Melt 2 tablespoons butter or margarine and brush over hens. Sprinkle with salt. Place remaining rice-stuffing mixture in aluminum-foil packet. Bake hens until tender, about 1-1/2 hours. Place packet of stuffing in baking pan in oven 30 minutes before end of baking time. Serve extra stuffing with hens. Makes 4 servings.

# Spiced Chicken

*You'll savor this unusual sweet-and-sour blend.*

2 tablespoons vegetable oil
3 lbs. chicken pieces
2 tablespoons brown sugar
2 teaspoons garlic salt
1-1/2 teaspoons oregano
1/4 teaspoon pepper
1/2 teaspoon cinnamon
2 tablespoons vinegar
1 bay leaf
4 medium carrots, cut in 3/4-inch chunks

3 medium onions, cut in wedges
1/2 cup pitted prunes, cut in half
1 cup UNCLE BEN'S® CONVERTED®
  Brand Rice
2-1/2 cups water
1 teaspoon salt
1 tablespoon butter or margarine
1 cup water
2 tablespoons flour
2 tablespoons chopped parsley

In a large skillet, heat oil. Add chicken and brown, turning to brown well on both sides. Sprinkle with brown sugar, garlic salt, oregano, pepper and cinnamon. Add vinegar, bay leaf, carrots, onions and prunes. Cover. Cook over low heat until chicken and vegetables are tender, about 45 minutes. Meanwhile, cook rice with 2-1/2 cups water, salt and butter or margarine, according to package directions. Remove chicken and vegetables from pan and keep warm. Skim off any excess fat from pan drippings. Combine 1 cup water and flour. Stir until free of lumps. Add to pan drippings. Cook until sauce is thickened, stirring constantly. Stir parsley into hot cooked rice. Remove bay leaf from chicken. Serve sauce with chicken over rice. Makes 6 servings.

# Sherried Chinese Chicken

*A secret ingredient brings out the best Chinese and Hawaiian flavors.*

1 (6-oz.) pkg. UNCLE BEN'S®
  Long Grain & Wild Rice
2-1/2 cups water
1 tablespoon butter or margarine
1 (20-oz.) can pineapple chunks
1/4 cup soy sauce
1/4 cup dry sherry
2 (9/16-oz.) packets Mai-Tai mix

2 cups cubed (1-1/2") cooked chicken
1 tablespoon vegetable oil
1 (16-oz.) can mixed Chinese vegetables, drained
1 cup frozen peas, thawed
1/2 cup slivered almonds
1 (4-oz.) can mushroom caps, drained
2 tablespoons sliced pimiento (1/2" x 1/4")
1 tablespoon cornstarch

Cook contents of rice and seasoning packets in water and butter or margarine according to package directions. Drain pineapple chunks; reserve 1/4 cup syrup. Combine reserved pineapple syrup, soy sauce, sherry and Mai-Tai mix. Pour over chicken. Refrigerate while preparing remaining ingredients. Heat oil in wok or large skillet. Add pineapple chunks, Chinese vegetables, peas, almonds, mushroom caps and pimiento. Pour 1/4 cup of chicken marinade into a small bowl. Add chicken and remaining marinade to wok or skillet. Stir and heat thoroughly. Combine the 1/4 cup marinade and cornstarch; stir until free of lumps. Add to chicken mixture. Cook until thickened and clear, about 5 minutes, stirring carefully. Serve over cooked rice. Makes 6 servings.

# Mexican Fruited Chicken

*Enjoy this tasty flavor combination with tortillas or taco chips.*

2 tablespoons vegetable oil
3 lbs. chicken pieces
1 medium onion, chopped
1 clove garlic, minced
1 teaspoon salt
1/4 teaspoon cinnamon
1/8 teaspoon ground cloves
1/8 teaspoon cayenne pepper
1/2 cup fresh orange juice
1 cup UNCLE BEN'S® CONVERTED®
  Brand Rice

2-1/2 cups water
1 teaspoon salt
1 tablespoon butter or margarine
1 (13-1/2-oz.) can pineapple tidbits
1 tablespoon cornstarch
1 tablespoon sugar
1/2 cup fresh orange juice
12 cherry tomatoes, cut in half
1 teaspoon grated orange peel
1 cup sliced celery

In a large skillet, heat oil. Add chicken. Brown, turning to brown well on both sides. Add onion and garlic. Sprinkle with salt, cinnamon, cloves and cayenne pepper. Add 1/2 cup of orange juice. Cover. Cook over low heat until chicken is tender, about 45 minutes. Meanwhile, cook rice with water, 1 teaspoon salt and 1 tablespoon butter or margarine according to package directions. When chicken is tender, remove from skillet; keep warm. Skim off any excess fat from pan drippings. Drain pineapple tidbits; reserve 1/2 cup syrup. In a small bowl, combine cornstarch and sugar. Add 1/2 cup orange juice and reserved pineapple syrup. Stir until free of lumps. Add to pan drippings. Cook until thickened, stirring constantly. Return chicken to skillet. Add pineapple tidbits and cherry tomatoes. Spoon sauce over top; sprinkle with orange peel. Stir celery into hot cooked rice; heat. Serve with chicken. Makes 6 servings.

# How To Make
## Plum-Glazed Chicken

Cook browned chicken over low heat, in a covered skillet until tender. Turn chicken several times while it's cooking.

After pouring sauce over chicken, continue to heat while spooning sauce over chicken until chicken is glazed and sauce is thick.

Serve the chicken and sauce over rice. Sprinkle with grated orange peel.

# Plum-Glazed Chicken

*Try this unusual gourmet combination.*

2 tablespoons butter or margarine
3 lbs. chicken pieces
2 tablespoons water
1/2 teaspoon salt
1/2 cup plum jelly
1/2 cup light corn syrup

1/4 cup orange juice
1 (6-oz.) pkg. UNCLE BEN'S®
   Long Grain & Wild Rice
2-1/2 cups water
1 tablespoon butter or margarine
2 teaspoons grated orange peel

In a large skillet, melt 2 tablespoons butter or margarine. Add chicken and brown. Add water and salt. Cover. Cook over low heat until tender, about 45 minutes, turning chicken several times. Drain fat from skillet. Combine jelly, corn syrup and orange juice, stir. Pour over chicken. Heat and spoon sauce over chicken until chicken is glazed and sauce is thickened, 5 to 10 minutes. Cook contents of rice and seasoning packets with water and 1 tablespoon butter or margarine according to package directions. Stir 1 teaspoon grated orange peel into hot cooked rice. Serve chicken and sauce over rice. Sprinkle with remaining teaspoon orange peel. Makes 6 servings.


# Mexican Arroz con Pollo

*Traditional Mexican vegetables highlight spicy chicken.*

2 tablespoons vegetable oil
2 cloves garlic, minced
3 lbs. chicken pieces
2 tablespoons flour
1 teaspoon salt
1/2 teaspoon ground cumin seed
1/4 teaspoon pepper
1 (1-1b.) can tomato wedges
1 medium onion, chopped

1 lb. zucchini, sliced 1/4-inch thick
1 teaspoon salt
1 cup UNCLE BEN'S® CONVERTED®
   Brand Rice
2-1/2 cups water
1 teaspoon salt
1 tablespoon butter or margarine
1 (7-oz.) can whole-kernel corn, drained

In a large skillet, heat oil and garlic. Brown chicken in oil, turning to brown well on both sides. Sprinkle chicken with flour, 1 teaspoon salt, cumin seed and pepper. Drain tomato wedges; reserve juice. Add onion and reserved tomato juice to chicken. Cover. Cook over low heat, about 30 minutes. Add zucchini, tomato wedges and 1 teaspoon salt. Cover. Cook until chicken and zucchini are tender, about 15 minutes. Skim off any excess fat. Cook rice with water, 1 teaspoon salt and 1 tablespoon butter or margarine according to package directions. Stir corn into hot cooked rice. Serve chicken with rice. Makes 6 servings.

# Islander's Lime Chicken

*Voyager's delight.*

2 tablespoons vegetable oil
3 lbs. chicken pieces
1 teaspoon salt
3/4 cup light corn syrup
1/2 cup golden or medium rum
1/4 cup lime juice
1 cup UNCLE BEN'S® CONVERTED®
   Brand Rice

2-1/2 cups water
1 teaspoon salt
1 tablespoon butter or margarine
1 tablespoon cornstarch
1 to 2 teaspoons grated lime peel
1 cup toasted flaked coconut

In a large skillet, heat oil. Add chicken and brown. Drain off fat. Sprinkle chicken with salt. Combine corn syrup, rum and lime juice. Spoon 2 tablespoons over chicken. Cover. Cook slowly until chicken is tender, about 45 minutes. Cook rice with water, salt and butter or margarine according to package directions. Remove chicken from skillet; keep warm. Spoon excess fat from drippings. Add cornstarch to remaining syrup mixture and add to drippings in skillet. Cook, stirring constantly, until sauce is clear and thickened, about 5 to 10 minutes. Pour sauce over chicken. Just before serving, sprinkle with lime peel. Sprinkle cooked rice with toasted coconut and serve with chicken. Makes 6 servings.

# Orange-Glazed Chicken & Peaches

*Brings sunshine to your table.*

2 tablespoons butter or margarine
3 lbs. chicken pieces
1/2 cup chopped onion
1 teaspoon salt
1/2 teaspoon ground ginger
1/2 teaspoon curry powder
1 (1-lb.-13-oz.) can sliced cling peaches
1/2 cup orange juice

1 tablespoon grated orange peel
1 tablespoon cornstarch
2 cups UNCLE BEN'S® QUICK™
   Brand Rice
1-2/3 cups water
1/2 teaspoon salt
1 tablespoon butter or margarine

In a large skillet, melt 2 tablespoons butter or margarine. Add chicken pieces. Brown well, turning to brown evenly. Add onion. Sprinkle with 1 teaspoon salt, ginger and curry powder. Drain sliced peaches; reserve 1/2 cup syrup and pour over chicken. Cover chicken. Cook over low heat until almost tender, about 35 minutes. Add sliced peaches. In a small bowl, combine orange juice, orange peel and cornstarch. Pour over chicken and peaches. Cover. Cook until chicken is tender and sauce thickened, about 10 minutes. Spoon sauce over chicken and peaches 2 or 3 times during cooking to glaze. Cook rice with water, 1/2 teaspoon salt and 1 tablespoon butter or margarine according to package directions. Serve chicken over hot cooked rice. Makes 4 servings.

**Variation:**
For a more subtle flavor, substitute 1/2 teaspoon paprika and 1/4 teaspoon thyme for ginger and curry powder.

# Zesty Chicken & Rice

*Easy because the seasonings are already mixed.*

3 lbs. chicken pieces
3/4 cup flour
1 (0.7-oz.) envelope garlic salad-dressing mix
2 tablespoons chili powder
1/4 cup vegetable oil
1 (10-oz.) can tomatoes

Water
1 medium onion, chopped
1 green pepper, chopped
1 cup UNCLE BEN'S® CONVERTED® Brand Rice
Salt and Pepper to taste

Wash and pat dry chicken. Place flour, salad-dressing mix and chili powder in paper or plastic bag. Add chicken and shake until coated with flour mixture. In a large skillet. heat oil. Add chicken and brown on all sides. Drain tomatoes, reserving juice. Add water to juice and make 2-1/2 cups liquid. Add tomatoes, liquid, onion, green pepper, rice, salt and pepper to chicken. Stir, making certain rice is covered with liquid. Bring to a boil. Reduce heat and cover. Cook over low heat until chicken is tender and liquid is absorbed, about 40 minutes. Makes 4 to 6 servings.

# Italian Chicken With Saffron Rice

*The quick and easy version.*

2 tablespoons vegetable oil or butter
2-1/2 to 3 lbs. chicken pieces
1/2 cup finely diced celery
1 small clove garlic, minced
2 tablespoons minced parsley
1 teaspoon salt

1 bay leaf, crumbled
1/2 cup Chablis or other dry white wine
1 tablespoon flour, if desired
1 tablespoon water, if desired
Quick Saffron Rice, see below

*Quick Saffron Rice:*
2 tablespoons butter or margarine
1/4 cup diced onion
1/16 teaspoon powdered saffron
1-1/2 cups chicken stock

2 cups UNCLE BEN'S® QUICK™ Brand Rice
1/2 teaspoon salt

In a large skillet, heat oil. Add chicken and brown on all sides. Add celery, garlic and parsley. Cook stirring vegetables, 2 minutes longer. Add salt, bay leaf and wine. Cover. Simmer until chicken is tender, about 40 minutes. If desired, thicken sauce with 1 tablespoon flour that has been blended with 1 tablespoon water. Serve with Quick Saffron Rice. Makes 4 servings.

**Quick Saffron Rice:**
In a large saucepan melt butter or margarine. Add onion. Cook until soft, but not brown. Add saffron and chicken stock; mix well. Stir in rice and salt. Bring to a *vigorous* boil and cover. Simmer until all liquid is absorbed, about 5 minutes.

# Seafood

Traditionally, seafood and rice have been favorites when served together. UNCLE BEN'S® kitchens have developed and perfected these recipes to help you prepare incredibly delicious seafood and rice. For a special family supper, serve Fisherman's-Wharf Casserole. It has something to please every-one. Sweet & Sour Shrimp is a perfect way to serve tender, succulent seafood. Tuna Creole Skillet is delicious, and won't strain your budget. Try Rainbow Trout with Mushroom Stuffing, or Baked Fish with Orange Stuffing.

*A Taste of the Sea*
* Fresh Shrimp Risotto
  Frenched Green Beans Almondine
  Avocado & Onion Salad
  Ice Cream

*Fisherman's Luck*
* Rainbow Trout with
    Mushroom Stuffing
  Broiled Tomatoes
  Creamed Spinach
  Hard Rolls & Butter
  Fruit Turnover

*Gourmet Dinner*
* Scallops with Glazed Walnuts
  Lemon-Buttered Asparagus
  Mixed Green Salad, Herb Dressing
  Strawberry Romanoff

*Budget Stretcher*
* Tuna Creole Skillet
  Buttered Corn
  Cole Slaw
  Lemon Cake

*Orient Express*
* Sweet & Sour Shrimp
  Sautéed Pea Pods & Onions
  Fresh Fruit Sherbet
  Cookies

*Family Pleaser*
* Fisherman's-Wharf Casserole
  Cut Green Beans & Onions
  Vegetable Relishes
  Apple Pie

*These recipes are in this section.*

# Fresh Shrimp Risotto

*Clam broth adds a hearty flavor.*

1 tablespoon finely chopped onion
3 tablespoons butter, melted
3/4 lb. fresh small shrimp, cleaned
  and deveined
2-1/2 cups chicken or clam broth

3 cups UNCLE BEN'S® QUICK™
  Brand Rice
1 teaspoon salt
1/4 teaspoon saffron
1/4 teaspoon ground pepper

In a medium skillet, cook onion in butter until golden. Add shrimp. Cook over medium heat until shrimp have golden color, about 4 to 5 minutes. Stir in remaining ingredients and bring to a *vigorous* boil. Cover and simmer until all liquid is absorbed, about 5 minutes. Serve hot. Makes 6 servings.

# Scallops With Glazed Walnuts

*Honey-glazed walnuts complement scallops in creamy sauce.*

1 cup UNCLE BEN'S® CONVERTED®
  Brand Rice
2-1/2 cups water
1 teaspoon salt
1 tablespoon butter or margarine
1/2 cup dry white wine
1/2 cup water
1/2 teaspoon salt
1 small bay leaf
1-1/2 lbs. scallops, fresh or frozen

4 tablespoons butter
3 green onions, sliced
3 tablespoons flour
Dash cayenne pepper
1 cup half and half
2 tablespoons butter
1/4 lb. fresh mushrooms sliced
2 tablespoons chopped parsley
Glazed Walnuts, see below

*Glazed Walnuts:*
1/4 cup honey

1/2 cup halved walnuts

Cook rice with 2-1/2 cups water, 1 teaspoon salt and 1 tablespoon butter or margarine according to package directions. While rice is cooking, combine wine, 1/2 cup water, salt and bay leaf in a medium saucepan. Bring to a boil. Cover and simmer 5 minutes. Add scallops and simmer about 4 to 5 minutes, or until tender. Remove scallops from liquid. Simmer liquid until it is reduced to about 3/4 cup. Remove bay leaf. Reserve liquid. In a large saucepan, melt 4 tablespoons butter. Sauté green onions until tender. Stir in flour and cayenne pepper. Gradually add half and half and scallop liquid. Cook, stirring constantly, until thickened. Add scallops. Melt 2 tablespoons butter in a small skillet. Sauté mushrooms until tender. Add parsley. Stir into cooked rice. Stir Glazed Walnuts into scallop mixture. Spoon scallops over hot cooked rice. Makes 6 servings.

Glazed Walnuts:
Place honey in a small skillet. Heat until mixture bubbles slightly. Add walnuts. Cook over low heat, keeping the honey bubbling slightly and stirring frequently, until walnuts are toasted and glazed, about 10 to 12 minutes. Keep warm.

# Fisherman's Wharf Casserole

*An adventure in taste!*

1 cup UNCLE BEN'S® CONVERTED®
  Brand Rice
2-1/2 cups water
1 teaspoon salt
1 tablespoon butter or margarine
1/2 cup sliced celery

1 (6-oz.) can pitted ripe olives, drained
  and cut in halves
2 tablespoons sliced green onion
1 cup mayonnaise
1 (6-1/2- or 7-oz.) can tuna, drained and flaked
1 (4-1/2-oz.) can shrimp, drained and rinsed

Cook rice with water, salt and butter or margarine according to package directions. Place rice in bowl; cover and refrigerate. Preheat oven to 350°F (177°C). Combine rice, celery, olives, green onion and mayonnaise. Mix well. Fold in tuna and shrimp. Spoon into shallow 1-1/2 quart casserole. Cover with aluminum foil, crimping it securely to edges of casserole. Bake until thoroughly heated, 25 to 30 minutes. Makes 4 to 6 servings.

# Fish Kebabs With Pineapple Sauce

*Delicious broiled on your outdoor grill.*

2 lbs. cod or other thick fish fillets,
  fresh or frozen, thawed
1 (15-1/4-oz.) can pineapple chunks in juice;
  reserve 1 cup juice for sauce
2 tablespoons butter or margarine, melted
1 teaspoon salt

2-1/2 cups Pineapple Barbecue Sauce,
  see below
3 cups UNCLE BEN'S® QUICK™
  Brand Rice
2-1/3 cups water
1-1/2 tablespoons butter or margarine
3/4 teaspoon salt

*Pineapple Barbecue Sauce:*
1 cup pineapple juice from pineapple chunks
3/4 cup catsup
1/2 cup chopped onion
1/4 cup vinegar

2 tablespoons light-brown sugar
1 tablespoon cornstarch
1/4 teaspoon ground ginger

Cut fish into 1-1/2-inch chunks. Thread fish chunks alternately with pineapple chunks onto 6 skewers. Arrange in a long shallow baking pan. Brush with melted butter or margarine. Sprinkle with salt. Spoon small amount of Pineapple Barbecue Sauce over fish. Broil 4 to 5 inches from heat, about 15 minutes, turning once. Brush with sauce several times during broiling. Cook rice with water, 1-1/2 tablespoons butter or margarine and 3/4 teaspoon salt according to package directions. Add remaining pineapple chunks to sauce. Serve kebabs on cooked rice. Spoon Pineapple Barbecue Sauce over both. Makes 6 servings.

**Pineapple Barbecue Sauce:**
Combine reserved pineapple juice, catsup, onion, vinegar, light-brown sugar, cornstarch and ginger. Stir until free of lumps. Cook until thickened, stirring constantly. Simmer, uncovered, to blend flavors, about 15 minutes. Makes about 2-1/2 cups.

# Stir-Fry Shrimp & Wild Rice

*Stir-frying brings out natural flavors.*

1 (6-1/4 oz.) pkg. UNCLE BEN'S®
   Fast Cooking Long Grain & Wild Rice
2 cups water
2 tablespoons butter or margarine
1 (8-oz.) can water chestnuts, drained
   and sliced
1 clove garlic, minced
1/2 teaspoon salt

2 tablespoons butter or margarine
2 tablespoons olive oil
1 tablespoon lemon juice
Dash of cayenne pepper
1 lb. shrimp, clean and deveined, fresh or frozen
2 green onions, sliced
1 tablespoon soy sauce

Cook contents of rice and seasoning packets with water and 2 tablespoons butter or margarine according to package directions. Stir water chestnuts into cooked rice. Mash garlic and salt together. Melt 2 tablespoons butter or margarine in a large skillet or wok. Add olive oil, lemon juice, garlic-salt mixture and cayenne pepper; heat. Add shrimp. Cook quickly until shrimp turns pink and flesh is white, 3 to 5 minutes. Stir in green onions and soy sauce. Serve over rice. Makes 6 servings.

# Scallops With Carnival Rice

*The secret ingredient is beer.*

1-1/2 lbs. fresh or frozen scallops
1/2 cup beer
1/2 teaspoon salt
1/8 teaspoon sugar
1 tablespoon catsup

2 tablespoons flour
2 tablespoons soft butter or margarine
1/2 cup chopped parsley
3 to 4 cups Carnival Rice, see below

Carnival Rice:
3 mushrooms, sliced
2 green onions, sliced
1 tablespoon butter or margarine
1 cup UNCLE BEN'S® CONVERTED®
   Brand Rice

2-1/2 cups chicken stock
1/2 teaspoon salt
4 cherry tomatoes, quartered
4 pitted ripe olives, quartered

Thaw fish, if frozen. Drain. About 15 minutes before rice is done, bring beer, salt and sugar to a boil in a medium saucepan. Add scallops. When mixture boils again, cover and reduce heat. Simmer 5 minutes or until scallops are done. Stir in catsup. Mix flour with butter or margarine to make smooth paste. Add to scallop mixture. Cook, stirring constantly, until sauce is smooth and thickened. Stir in parsley. Spoon scallops and sauce over servings of rice. Makes 4 servings.

Carnival Rice:
In a medium skillet, sauté mushrooms and green onions in butter or margarine about 2 minutes. Add rice, chicken stock and salt. Bring to a boil and cover. Simmer 20 minutes. Remove from heat. Let stand until all liquid has been absorbed, about 5 minutes. Add tomatoes and ripe olives. Mix gently.

# Sole Roll-Ups With Sweet-Sour Sauce

*A festive fruit-vegetable blend.*

2 lbs. (12 small) sole or other thin
  fillets, fresh or frozen
1 teaspoon salt
1/8 teaspoon white pepper
1-1/2 cups shredded carrot
2 tablespoons chopped green onion
1/4 cup butter or margarine

1 cup UNCLE BEN'S® CONVERTED®
  Brand Rice
2-1/2 cups water
1 teaspoon salt
1 tablespoon butter or margarine
2-1/2 cups Sweet-Sour Sauce, see below

*Sweet-Sour Sauce:*
1 (12-oz.) can pineapple juice
2 tablespoons vinegar
2 tablespoons light-brown sugar

2 tablespoons cornstarch
1 teaspoon soy sauce
2 tablespoons green onion

Thaw fish, if frozen. Preheat oven to 350°F (177°C). Sprinkle 1 teaspoon salt and white pepper evenly over fillets. Cook carrot and green onion in 2 tablespoons of butter or margarine over low heat until carrots are tender, about 10 minutes. Spread an equal amount of carrot mixture on each fillet and roll up. Place in 12" x 8" baking dish, open side down. Melt remaining 2 tablespoons butter or margarine and drizzle over fish rolls. Bake until fish flakes easily when tested with a fork, 25 to 30 minutes. Cook rice with water, 1 teaspoon salt and 1 tablespoon butter or margarine according to package directions. Serve fish on rice and spoon Sweet-Sour Sauce over all. Makes 6 servings.

Sweet-Sour Sauce:

Combine pineapple juice, vinegar, brown sugar, cornstarch and soy sauce. Stir until free of lumps. Cook until clear and thickened, stirring constantly. Stir in remaining green onion. Makes 2-1/2 cups.

**Stir pineapple juice, vinegar, brown sugar, cornstarch and soy sauce until no lumps remain. Add green onion after sauce thickens and becomes clear.**

**Divide carrot mixture into twelve equal portions. Spread a portion on each fillet and roll up.**

# Cod Italiano

*Try this zesty, protein-packed casserole.*

2 lbs. cod or other thick fish fillets,
    fresh or frozen
1 teaspoon salt
1/2 teaspoon oregano
1 (15-1/2-oz.) jar spaghetti sauce
    with mushrooms
1 cup UNCLE BEN'S® CONVERTED®
    Brand Rice

2-1/2 cups water
1 teaspoon salt
1 tablespoon butter or margarine
1 cup shredded mozzarella cheese
1/4 cup grated Parmesan cheese
1/2 teaspoon oregano
1/4 cup sliced green onion

Thaw fish, if frozen. Preheat oven to 350°F (177°C). Cut fish into 6 serving portions. Arrange fish in 10" x 6" baking dish. Sprinkle with 1 teaspoon salt and 1/2 teaspoon oregano. Pour spaghetti sauce over fish. Bake until fish flakes easily when tested with a fork, 30 to 40 minutes. Cook rice with water, 1 teaspoon salt and butter or margarine according to package directions. Sprinkle cooked fish with mozzarella and Parmesan cheese. Sprinkle 1/2 teaspoon oregano over top. Return to oven to melt cheese, about 5 minutes. Stir green onion into rice. Serve fish and sauce over hot cooked rice. Makes 6 servings.

# Baked Fish With Orange Stuffing

*Fresh orange segments give a refreshing touch.*

1-1/2 cups UNCLE BEN'S® QUICK™
    Brand Rice
1 cup water
1/3 cup orange-juice concentrate
1/4 cup chopped onion
2 tablespoons butter or margarine
1/2 teaspoon salt

1 cup sliced celery
1/2 cup chopped toasted almonds
3 to 4 lbs. fish, sea or lake trout, whitefish or
    other fish, boned for stuffing
1 teaspoon salt
2 tablespoons butter or margarine, melted

Preheat oven to 350°F (177°C). Butter or oil a large shallow baking pan that will hold the fish. In a large saucepan, combine rice, water, orange-juice concentrate, onion, butter or margarine and 1/2 teaspoon salt; stir. Bring to a boil. Cover and simmer until all liquid is absorbed, about 5 minutes. Stir in celery and almonds. Clean, wash and dry fish. Sprinkle cavity with 1 teaspoon salt. Place in baking pan. Fill fish with rice mixture. Brush fish with melted butter or margarine. Cover with aluminum foil. Bake until fish flakes easily when tested with a fork, 30 to 40 minutes. Makes 6 servings.

# Scampi Rice

*For dinner-time drama, do the final steps at the table.*

1 small onion, sliced
1 tablespoon olive oil
1 (6-oz.) pkg. UNCLE BEN'S®
  Long Grain & Wild Rice
1 (1-lb.) can tomato wedges
Water

2 cloves garlic, finely diced
3 tablespoons butter or margarine
2 lbs. large shrimp, cleaned and
  deveined, fresh or frozen
1/4 cup dry white wine
2 tablespoons chopped parsley

In a large saucepan, sauté onion in olive oil until tender, but not brown. Add contents of rice and seasoning packets. Mix well. Drain tomato wedges; reserve liquid. Add water to tomato liquid to make 2-1/4 cups; add with wedges to rice mixture. Bring to a boil and cover. Simmer until rice is tender and liquid has been absorbed, about 25 minutes. In a medium skillet or wok, sauté garlic in butter or margarine until tender, but not brown. Add shrimp. Cook over high heat, stirring frequently, until shrimp are opaque. Add wine and continue cooking 5 minutes. Sprinkle with parsley. Serve shrimp and sauce over cooked rice. Makes 8 servings.

# Creamy Curried Shrimp With Coconut Rice

*A deliciously exotic dish.*

1 cup UNCLE BEN'S® CONVERTED®
  Brand Rice
2-1/2 cups water
1 teaspoon salt
1 tablespoon butter or margarine
1/2 cup flaked coconut, toasted,
  if desired
1 medium onion, chopped
1 medium apple, peeled and chopped
1 clove garlic, minced
1/4 cup butter or margarine

1 tablespoon curry powder, or to taste.
2 tablespoons flour
1-1/2 teaspoons salt
1/4 teaspoon ground ginger
2 cups half and half
1/2 cup milk
1 lb. cooked shrimp
1 tablespoon lemon juice
1 or 2 bananas, peeled, quartered lengthwise
  and cut in 1-in.-thick pieces, if desired
Chutney, if desired

Cook rice with water, 1 teaspoon salt and 1 tablespoon butter or margarine according to package directions. Stir coconut into hot cooked rice, if desired. In a large skillet, cook onion, apple and garlic in 1/4 cup butter or margarine until onion is tender, but not brown. Add curry powder. Stir. Cook 2 to 3 minutes, being careful curry powder does not burn. Stir in flour, 1-1/2 teaspoons salt and ginger. Add half and half and milk. Cook until sauce is thickened, stirring constantly. Add shrimp and lemon juice. Heat thoroughly. Serve rice with the shrimp sauce. Top with chopped banana and chutney, if desired. Makes 6 servings.

# Sweet & Sour Shrimp

*Quick-cooked shrimp retain their naturally sweet flavor.*

1 cup UNCLE BEN'S® CONVERTED®
  Brand Rice
2-1/2 cups water
1 teaspoon salt
1 tablespoon butter or margarine
1 lb. fresh shrimp, cleaned and
  deveined
1 tablespoon soy sauce
1/2 teaspoon salt

About 1/2 cup cornstarch
About 2 to 3 cups vegetable oil
1 tablespoon vegetable oil
1 small onion, cut in thin wedges
1 small green pepper, cut in chunks
1 cup Sweet & Sour Sauce, see below
1 cup canned pineapple chunks in unsweetened
  juice; reserve 1/2 cup juice for sauce
2 small tomatoes, cut in thin wedges

*Sweet & Sour Sauce:*
1 cup sugar
2 tablespoons cornstarch
4 teaspoons salt
1 cup red-wine vinegar

1/2 cup orange juice
1/2 cup pineapple juice (drained from
  pineapple chunks)
1 (6-oz.) can tomato paste

Cook rice with water, 1 teaspoon salt and butter or margarine according to package directions. Combine shrimp, soy sauce and salt; mix well. Coat shrimp evenly with cornstarch. Heat 2 to 3 cups oil to 350°F (177°C). In a large skillet or wok, deep-fat fry shrimp in oil until shrimp is firm and cooked, about 3 minutes. Do not overcook. Drain on paper towel. Keep warm in very low oven, 250°F (121°C). In a large skillet or wok, stir 1 tablespoon vegetable oil, onion and green pepper just until heated. Add 1 cup Sweet & Sour Sauce and pineapple chunks. Heat thoroughly. Carefully stir in shrimp and tomato wedges. Cook until mixture is heated and coated with sauce. Spoon Sweet & Sour Shrimp over hot cooked rice. Makes 4 servings.

### Sweet & Sour Sauce:
Blend sugar, cornstarch and salt. Stir in vinegar, orange juice, pineapple juice and tomato paste. Cook, stirring constantly, until thickened and glossy. Cover and refrigerate 2 cups of sauce to use at another time. Makes 3 cups of sauce.

### Variations:
To make Sweet & Sour Pork, substitute 1 pound of lean boneless pork, cut into 3/4-inch cubes, for shrimp. Deep-fat fry pork until thoroughly cooked, 3 to 5 minutes.

To make Sweet & Sour Chicken, substitute 1-1/2 pounds chicken breasts for shrimp. Bone uncooked chicken, remove skin and cut into 3/4-inch cubes. Deep-fat fry until chicken turns white and is thoroughly cooked, 3 to 5 minutes.

# Tuna Creole Skillet

*Easy and economical.*

1/2 cup chopped green pepper
2 tablespoons butter or margarine
1 (1-lb.) can stewed tomatoes
1 cup UNCLE BEN'S® CONVERTED®
   Brand Rice

1-1/4 teaspoons salt
1 tablespoon instant minced onion
1 (6-1/2 or 7-oz.) can tuna, drained and flaked

In a large skillet, sauté green pepper in butter or margarine 2 or 3 minutes. Drain tomatoes, reserving juice. Add water to juice to make 2-1/2 cups liquid. Add tomatoes, liquid, rice, salt and onion to skillet; stir. Bring to a boil. Cover and simmer 20 minutes. Remove from heat. Let stand, covered, until all liquid is absorbed, about 5 minutes. Fold in tuna and heat through. Makes 4 to 6 servings.

Variations:
Sauté sliced fresh mushroom with green pepper.
Substitute 1/4 cup dry white wine for 1/4 cup of the liquid.
Substitute cooked shrimp for tuna fish.

# Scallops & Wild Rice

*Tender scallops in a delicate egg sauce.*

1-1/2 lbs. fresh or frozen scallops
1 (6-oz.) pkg. UNCLE BEN'S®
   Long Grain & Wild Rice
2-1/2 cups water
1 tablespoon butter or margarine
Cold water
2 tablespoons butter or margarine

1/3 cup sherry
1 teaspoon salt
1 cup half and half or light cream
3 egg yolks, beaten
1 (2-oz.) jar sliced pimiento, drained
2 tablespoons coarsely chopped parsley

Thaw fish, if frozen. Cook contents of rice and seasoning packets with 2-1/2 cups water and 1 tablespoon butter or margarine according to package directions. While rice cooks, place scallops in chafing-dish pan or top of double boiler over direct heat. Cover with cold water; bring to a boil. Remove from heat and drain. Add 2 tablespoons butter or margarine and cook, stirring constantly, for 3 minutes after butter has melted. Place over boiling water. Add sherry, salt and half and half. Heat. Gradually stir 1/2 cup of hot mixture into egg yolks. Mix well. Stir egg-yolk-and-sauce mixture into scallops. Cook, stirring constantly, until sauce is smooth and thickened. Add pimiento and parsley. Serve at once over cooked rice. Makes 4 servings.

# Wild Rice Oyster Bake

*A delicacy-filled casserole!*

1 (6-oz.) pkg. UNCLE BEN'S®
  Long Grain & Wild Rice
1/4 teaspoon salt
1 cup sliced fresh mushrooms
1/2 cup sliced leeks
2 tablespoons butter or margarine

1 (10-oz.) can frozen oysters, thawed
  and drained, or 1/2 pt. fresh oysters,
  drained
1-1/4 cups water
1 cup half and half
Chopped parsley

Preheat oven to 375°F (191°C). Place contents or rice and seasoning packets with salt in a 1-1/2 quart casserole. Cook mushrooms and leeks in butter or margarine until mushrooms are tender. Add oysters. Cook until edges curl. Add water and bring to a boil. Stir in half and half. Pour over rice mixture. Mix and cover. Bake for 30 minutes. Uncover and stir. Bake, uncovered, 5 minutes longer. Sprinkle with parsley. Makes 6 to 8 servings.

**Variation:**
Substitute green onions for leeks.

# Rainbow Trout With Mushroom Stuffing

*Garnish with slices of tangy lemon and sprigs of crisp parsley.*

6 (8-oz.) pan-dressed rainbow trout,
  or other small fish, boned for stuffing,
  fresh or frozen
1 (6-oz.) pkg. UNCLE BEN'S®
  Long Grain & Wild Rice
2-1/2 cups water
1 tablespoon butter or margarine

1 cup sliced mushrooms
1/4 cup sliced green onion
2 tablespoons butter or margarine
2 tablespoons chopped pimiento
1 tablespoon lemon juice
1 teaspoon salt
2 tablespoons butter or margarine, if desired

Thaw fish, if frozen. Preheat oven to 350°F (177°C). Cook contents of rice and seasoning packets with water and 1 tablespoon butter or margarine according to package directions. Cook mushrooms and green onion in 2 tablespoons butter or margarine until mushrooms are tender, not brown. Stir into cooked rice. Stir in pimiento and lemon juice. Sprinkle inside of fish with salt. Fill fish cavities with equal amounts of rice mixture, about 1/2 cup each. Arrange fish in single layer in baking pan. Brush with 2 tablespoons melted butter or margarine, if desired. Bake until fish flakes easily when tested with a fork, 25 to 30 minutes. Makes 6 servings.

# Entertaining

With recipes in this section you can create elegant meals like the Paella pictured on the cover of this book. For a delectable brunch, serve Quiche Oriental. Curried Buffet Meatballs will be a success at your next buffet. Rice is a delectable base for a variety of sauces from hearty, home-style Beef Rolls With Creamy Mushroom Sauce to the delicious gourmet flavors of Surf & Turf Rice. Keep UNCLE BEN'S® Rice in mind for the starting point of your week-end brunch, a leisurely lunch or a superb holiday dinner.

*French Riviera Brunch*
* Oriental Quiche
  Peas and Mushrooms
  Assorted Cheeses
  French Bread
  Poached Pears

*A Memorable Dinner*
* Lamb Mesheke
  Buttered Mixed Cauliflower &
     Broccoli Buds
  Peach Melba

*The Male Vote*
* Beef Rolls with
     Creamy Mushroom Sauce
  Zucchini & Cherry Tomatoes
  Chocolate Brownies a la Mode

*The Boss Is Invited To Dinner*
  Paté & French Bread
* Paella
  Bibb & Romaine Salad
  Wine Vinegar-Oil Dressing
  Lemon Soufflé

*Hearty Harvest Dinner*
* Cranberried Duck with
     Wild Rice Stuffing
  Baked Squash
  Buttered Brussels Sprouts
  Apple Tarts

*"It's A Come and Go Buffet"*
* Curried Buffet Meatballs
  Sliced Roast Turkey
  Broccoli Almondine
  Cold Cooked Vegetables
  Assorted Breads
  Roquefort Cheese
  Chocolate Cake
  Bowl of Mixed Fruit

*These recipes are in this section.*

# Vegetable-Rice Ring

*A new version of refreshing gazpacho.*

1-1/2 cups *cooked* and chilled UNCLE
   BEN'S® CONVERTED® Brand Rice
1/2 cup Italian salad dressing
1/3 cup mayonnaise
1-1/4 cups seeded and chopped tomato
3/4 cup sliced radishes
3/4 cup seeded and chopped cucumber

1/4 cup chopped green pepper
1/4 cup chopped celery
1/4 cup chopped green onion
Leaf lettuce
1 pt. cherry tomatoes
1 medium cucumber, thinly sliced

Lightly coat a 4-1/2-cup ring mold with mayonnaise. Combine chilled rice and Italian salad dressing. Marinate 4 to 6 hours or overnight. Add mayonnaise and mix well. Fold in chopped tomato, radishes, chopped cucumber, green pepper, celery and onion. Press into prepared ring mold. Cover and chill 2 to 3 hours. Invert to unmold on lettuce-lined serving plate. Fill center with cherry tomatoes and surround ring with overlapping slices of cucumber. Makes 6 servings.

# Braised Rice-Stuffed Lamb

*A superb holiday roast.*

1 (6-oz.) pkg. UNCLE BEN'S®
   Long Grain & Wild Rice
2-1/2 cups water
1 tablespoon butter or margarine
4-1/2 to 5-lb. lamb cushion
   shoulder roast
3 tablespoons peanut or
   vegetable oil
2 large onions, minced
2 cloves garlic, crushed and minced
1/2 lb. pork sausage
1 teaspoon thyme

10 to 15 sprigs parsley, minced
1 large carrot, peeled and minced
1 celery stalk, minced
2 eggs, slightly beaten
2 teaspoons salt
Freshly ground pepper to taste
Salt and pepper for seasoning
5 tablespoons peanut or vegetable oil
1 cup dry white wine
1 cup chicken broth
1 tablespoon tomato paste

Preheat oven to 325°F (163°C). Cook contents of rice and seasoning packets with water and butter or margarine according to package directions. Make a pocket in the meat. Heat 3 tablespoons oil in a heavy, large skillet. Add half the minced onion and all the garlic. Sauté for 2 minutes. Add sausage; cook until no longer pink. Stir in the rice, thyme, parsley, 1/2 of the minced carrot, all the celery, eggs, 2 teaspoons salt and pepper to taste. Cook for another 2 minutes. Season the meat pocket with salt and pepper. Stuff with the rice-vegetable mixture, making certain to fill the corners. Secure the opening with skewers. Pour 2 tablespoons of the oil in a 3-quart (13-1/2" x 8-1/2" x 2") baking dish. Add the meat. Salt and pepper the outside to taste and pour the remaining 3 tablespoons of oil over meat. Scatter remaining onion and carrot around meat. Combine wine, broth and tomato paste and pour over meat. Bake for 2 hours, to an internal temperature of 175°F (79°C). Baste the meat regularly with the pan juices. Do not pierce the meat or turn it over. Remove the meat to a serving platter and keep warm. Strain the juices from the baking dish and serve with the meat. Makes 6 to 8 servings.

# Surf & Turf Rice

*Delicacies galore!*

1 lb. boneless steak, cut in
   1-in. cubes
1 tablespoon butter
4 (5 to 6-oz.) rock-lobster tails,
   cut in 1-in. slices
2 tablespoons butter
1 tablespoon dry white wine
1 teaspoon lemon juice

Water
3 cups sliced mushrooms
3 green onions and tops, sliced
2 tablespoons butter or margarine
3 cups UNCLE BEN'S® QUICK™
   Brand Rice
Sherry-Butter Sauce, see below

*Sherry-Butter Sauce:*

2 tablespoons butter
1 clove garlic, crushed
1/2 cup medium sherry

1/4 cup chopped parsley
1/2 teaspoon meat-extract paste
   or 1 teaspoon bouillon granules

In a large skillet, sauté steak cubes in 1 tablespoon butter until browned on all sides, turning often. Put into a large bowl; set aside. Clean skillet. Sauté lobster-tail slices in 2 tablespoons butter, stirring often, until opaque. Add wine and lemon juice. Cover. Simmer 5 minutes. Remove lobster slices; set aside. Pour liquid from skillet into measuring cup; add water to make 2-1/4 cups; reserve for rice. In a medium saucepan, sauté mushrooms and green onions in 2 tablespoons butter or margarine for 6 minutes, stirring often. Add reserved lobster liquid and water. Add rice. Bring to a boil. Cover and simmer until all liquid is absorbed, about 5 minutes. Combine lobster-tail slices with steak cubes and warm thoroughly. Serve on hot rice. Spoon hot Sherry-Butter Sauce over servings. Makes 6 servings.

Sherry-Butter Sauce:
In small saucepan heat all sauce ingredients until bubbling.

Variation:
Substitute 1-1/2 lbs. fresh or thawed frozen scallops for rock-lobster tails.

# Baked Rice & Cheese Italiano

*Unique flavor in an easily assembled casserole.*

1-1/2 cups UNCLE BEN'S® CONVERTED®
  Brand Rice
1-1/2 cups dry white wine
1 (1-lb.) can tomatoes, cut up
1 (13-3/4-oz.) can chicken broth
2 medium zucchini, sliced 1/2-inch thick
2 medium onions, sliced
1 cup water
1/4 cup butter or margarine

2 teaspoons salt
2 teaspoons minced garlic
1 teaspoon basil
1/4 teaspoon pepper
1 bay leaf
1 cup shredded sharp Cheddar cheese
1 cup shredded Romano cheese
1 cup whipping cream

Preheat oven to 400°F (205°C). Combine all ingredients except cheeses and cream in a 13-1/2" x 8-1/2" baking dish; mix. Cover with aluminum foil, crimping it tightly to edges of dish. Bake 1 hour, stirring at the end of 30 minutes. Uncover. Stir in cheeses and cream. Return to oven. Continue baking, uncovered, 10 minutes longer. Makes 8 to 10 servings.

# Seafood Jambalaya

*Pickling spices blend superbly with fish and vegetables for a piquant flavor.*

1-1/2 cups diced onions
1/4 cup olive oil
1 cup finely diced celery
4 cups chopped tomatoes
1/2 cup dry white wine
1 teaspoon paprika
2 tablespoons tomato paste
4 bay leaves
1 tablespoon pickling spice in
  cheesecloth bag, see below

2 teaspoons salt
1/8 teaspoon cayenne pepper
6 fresh oysters
15 medium size fresh shrimp,
  cleaned and deveined
1/2 cup diced fresh scallops
1-1/2 cups UNCLE BEN'S® CONVERTED®
  Brand Rice
3 cups boiling water

Preheat oven to 375°F (191°C). In large saucepan with heatproof handles and cover, cook onions in olive oil until golden. Add celery. Cook until softened. Stir in tomatoes, wine and paprika. Bring to a boil. Add tomato paste, bay leaves, pickling spice in cheesecloth bag, salt and cayenne pepper, bring to a boil. Stir in remaining ingredients. Cover tightly and bake for 40 to 45 minutes or until almost all water is absorbed. Remove cheesecloth bag and bay leaves. For each serving, fill soup cup or individual bowl with jambalaya, press lightly and unmold on plate. Serve hot. Makes 6 servings.

To make cheesecloth bag with pickling spice, cut double thickness of cheesecloth into 7-inch square; place pickling spice in center. Gather edges together and tie with string.

**Variations:**
Substitute 1 (6-oz.) can whole oysters, drained, for fresh oysters.
Substitute frozen shimp and scallops for fresh.

# Paella

*Festive memories of Spain.*

1 (1-1/4 lbs.) lobster or 2
   (8- to 10-oz.) lobster tails
4 tablespoons olive oil
5 small chicken breasts, halved
   and boned
4 tablespoons olive oil, if needed
3 medium onions, chopped
1 clove garlic, minced
3 large tomatoes, chopped, or
   1 (1-lb.) can tomatoes, drained
3 medium green or red peppers,
   chopped
2 cups UNCLE BEN'S® CONVERTED®
   Brand Rice

2 (13-3/4-oz.) cans chicken broth
1 cup dry white wine.
3 teaspoons salt
1/2 teaspoon leaf thyme
1/2 teaspoon oregano
1/4 teaspoon ground coriander
1/4 teaspoon saffron
1/4 teaspoon paprika
1 bay leaf
10 to 12 large shrimp (about 1/2 lb.)
   cleaned and deveined
12 little neck clams or mussels
1 lb. Spanish or Mexican sausage (chorizo)
1/2 cup frozen peas, thawed

If using whole lobster, remove tail and claws; cut into 3 or 4 pieces each. If using lobster tails, cut into 5 or 6 pieces each. Heat 4 tablespoons of oil in a large paella pan, electric skillet or two 12-inch skillets. Add lobster pieces. Sauté 3 minutes. Remove lobster and set aside. Sauté chicken until well browned on both sides, adding more oil if needed. Remove chicken pieces and set aside. Sauté onions and garlic until tender, but not brown. Add tomatoes and green or red peppers. Cook until tender and most of the liquid has evaporated. Add rice, broth and wine. Stir in salt, thyme, oregano, coriander, saffron, paprika and bay leaf. Mix well and bring to a boil. Arrange chicken pieces in center and place lobster pieces and shrimp around edge of pan. Add clams or mussels. Cook until shells open. Remove clams or mussels from water; set aside. Remove casing from sausage; slice thinly. Add clams or mussels and sausage slices to rice mixture. Sprinkle with peas. Cover. Cook until liquid is absorbed, about 10 minutes. Remove cover to allow excess moisture to evaporate, if needed. Remove bay leaf. Makes 10 servings.

Variation:
Increase shrimp to 1 pound and omit lobster and clams or mussels.

**Paella**

# Curried Apricot Pork With Pecan Rice

*Lazy gourmet cooks enjoy putting this one together.*

1 (8-3/4-oz.) can apricot halves in syrup
2 tablespoons butter or margarine
1-1/2 lbs. lean boneless pork,
   cut in 1-inch cubes
1 medium onion, chopped
2 teaspoons curry powder
1 teaspoon salt
Dash of cayenne pepper

1 tablespoon vinegar
1 cup UNCLE BEN'S® CONVERTED®
   Brand Rice
2-1/2 cups water
1 teaspoon salt
1 tablespoon butter or margarine
1/2 cup coarsely chopped pecans

Place apricot halves and syrup in blender container. Cover and puree until smooth. If you don't have a blender, mash with a fork. Heat butter or margarine in a large skillet. Add pork; brown well on all sides. Add onion, curry powder, salt and cayenne pepper. Stir. Cook 2 to 3 minutes, being careful curry powder does not burn. Add pureed apricots and vinegar. Stir and cover. Cook over low heat until meat is tender, 1 to 1-1/4 hours, stirring several times. Cook rice with water, 1 teaspoon salt and 1 tablespoon butter or margarine according to package directions. Stir pecans into hot cooked rice. Serve with pork. Makes 6 servings.

# Curried Buffet Meatballs

*Unusual sauce adds spice to a traditional favorite.*

2 medium onions, chopped
1 lb. ground beef
1/4 cup milk
1 egg
1/2 teaspoon salt
1 (6-oz.) pkg. UNCLE BEN'S®
   Long Grain & Wild Rice
2 tablespoons butter or margarine
2 tablespoons flour

1/3 cup seedless raisins
1/2 teaspoon curry powder
1/4 teaspoon cinnamon
3-1/2 cups water
1 tablespoon butter
1 teaspoon salt
Flaked coconut, if desired
Slivered almonds, if desired

Measure 1/2 cup chopped onions. In a large mixing bowl, combine 1/2 cup chopped onions, ground beef, milk, eggs, 1/2 teaspoon salt and seasoning packet from rice. Mix well. Shape into 24 balls. In a large skillet, melt 2 tablespoons butter or margarine and sauté remaining onions until tender. Stir in flour, raisins, curry powder and cinnamon. Cook and stir 2 to 3 minutes. Gradually add 1 cup water. Cook, stirring constantly, until thickened. Add meatballs and cover. Cook over low heat, stirring occasionally, until meat is done, about 30 minutes. In a large saucepan, combine remaining 2-1/2 cups water, 1 tablespoon butter and 1 teaspoon salt. Add contents of rice packet. Bring to a boil and cover tightly. Simmer 25 minutes. Serve with meatballs and sauce. Before serving, sprinkle with flaked coconut or slivered almonds, if desired. Makes 4 to 6 servings.

Shape ground-beef mixture into 24 balls.

# *How to Make*
# *Curried Buffet Meatballs*

Add meatballs to curry mixture in skillet. Cover. Cook,
stirring occasionally.

Serve curried meatballs and sauce over rice. Sprinkle with
flaked coconut or slivered almonds, if desired.

# Sausage-Apricot Pastry Logs

*Gourmet cooking with easy, frozen patty shells.*

1 (6-oz.) pkg. UNCLE BEN'S®
  Long Grain & Wild Rice
2-1/2 cups water
1 tablespoon butter or margarine
1 lb. pork sausage
1 (1-lb.) can apricot halves

2 tablespoons sugar
2 teaspoons cornstarch
1/4 teaspoon nutmeg
2 tablespoons lemon juice
1 (10-oz.) pkg. frozen patty shells,
  thawed

Preheat oven to 400°F (205°C). Cook contents of rice and seasoning packets with water and butter or margarine according to package directions. Brown sausage until crumbly; drain well. Drain apricot halves; reserve syrup. Dice apricot halves; reserve 1/2 cup for sauce. In a medium saucepan, combine sugar, cornstarch and nutmeg. Mix. Stir in apricot syrup, reserved 1/2 cup diced apricots and lemon juice. Cook over moderate heat until sauce is thickened, stirring constantly. In a large bowl, combine cooked rice, sausage, remaining diced apricots and 1/4 cup of sauce. Mix lightly. Roll each patty shell on lightly floured board into a 7-inch circle. Moisten edges lightly with water. Spoon about 1 cup of filling in a strip down center of pastry. Fold sides of pastry over filling; seal. Place logs, seam side down, on ungreased baking sheet. Bake until lightly browned, about 25 minutes. Serve with remaining sauce. Makes 6 servings.

# Mile-High Treasure Pie

*Has everything but Jack Horner's plum!*

10 slices bacon, diced
1 cup *cooked* UNCLE BEN'S®
  Long Grain & Wild Rice
1 (9-inch) unbaked pastry shell with
  2-in.-high fluted edge
1 large tomato, sliced
1 medium green pepper, cut in thin
  strips

1/2 cup shredded Cheddar cheese
1/2 cup shredded process American cheese
3 eggs, separated
3/4 cup dairy sour cream
1/2 cup flour
1/4 cup grated Parmesan cheese
Garlic salt to taste
Paprika for garnish

Preheat oven to 350°F (177°C). Sauté bacon until lightly browned, stirring often. Drain on paper toweling. Spoon cooked rice over bottom of pastry shell. Arrange tomato slices, green pepper, 1/2 of the bacon and shredded cheeses in 1 layer each. Top with remaining bacon. Beat egg yolks; stir in sour cream, flour and Parmesan cheese. Beat whites until they hold soft peaks. Carefully fold egg whites into egg-yolk mixture. Pour over bacon layer. Sprinkle with garlic salt and paprika. Bake until table knife inserted in center comes out clean, 40 to 45 minutes. Makes 4 to 6 servings.

# Lamb Mesheke

*Easy and exotic.*

1/3 cup vegetable oil
2 lbs. boneless lamb, cut into 1-1/2-in.
  cubes
3 medium onions, chopped
3 cloves garlic, minced
2 teaspoons salt

1/2 to 1 teaspoon crushed red pepper
1 teaspoon turmeric
2/3 cup seedless raisins
1/3 cup dry sherry
4 to 5 tomatoes, peeled and chopped
Rice Mesheke, see below

*Rice Mesheke:*
1 cup UNCLE BEN'S® CONVERTED®
  Brand Rice
2-1/2 cups water
1 teaspoon salt
1 tablespoon butter or margarine
1 small onion, chopped
2/3 cup slivered or chopped almonds
  or pine nuts

1/3 cup olive oil
1/2 teaspoon paprika
1/4 teaspoon hot pepper sauce, if
  desired
Chopped parsley
Chopped pimiento

In a large skillet, heat oil. Add lamb and brown all surfaces. Add onions and garlic. Cook until onion is tender, but not brown, stirring frequently. Add salt, red pepper and turmeric. Mix well and cover. Cook over low heat until meat is tender, about 1-1/2 to 2 hours, stirring frequently. In a small saucepan combine raisins and sherry. Bring to a simmer over medium heat and cover. Let stand about 30 minutes, or until ready to use. Stir raisin-sherry mixture and tomatoes into meat mixture. Heat thoroughly. Serve over Rice Mesheke with bowl of condiments. Makes 6 servings.

**Rice Mesheke:**
Cook rice with water, salt and butter or margarine according to package directions. In a medium saucepan, sauté onion and nuts in oil until nuts are lightly browned. Stir in hot cooked rice, paprika and hot pepper sauce, if desired. Garnish with chopped parsley and pimiento.

**Condiments:**
Toasted almonds, fried onion rings and chopped fresh parsley.

**Variation:**
Substitute beef for lamb.

# Beef Rolls With Creamy Mushroom Sauce

*Split flank steaks make a hearty beef roll.*

1 (6-oz.) pkg. UNCLE BEN'S®
   Long Grain & Wild Rice
2-1/2 cups water
1 tablespoon butter or margarine
1 (10-3/4-oz.) can condensed
   cream-of-mushroom soup
2 tablespoons chopped pimiento
2 (1-lb.) flank steaks

2 teaspoons salt
1/4 teaspoon pepper
2 tablespoons shortening, melted
1/2 cup water
1/4 lb. mushrooms, sliced
1/2 cup half and half
1/4 teaspoon paprika

Cook contents of rice and seasoning packets with water and 1 tablespoon butter or margarine according to package directions. Stir 1/2 cup condensed soup and pimiento into cooked rice. With a long, sharp knife, slit each flank steak horizontally from one long side to within 1/2 inch of the other. Open and lay flat. Pound slightly to flatten evenly. Sprinkle with salt and pepper. Spread each steak with rice mixture, leaving outer 1 inch free. Carefully roll up each steak with the grain lengthwise, jelly-roll fashion. Fasten together securely with metal skewers or tie with cord. In a large skillet, brown rolls in shortening, turning carefully to brown all sides. Add 1/4 cup water; cover tightly and cook over low heat until meat is tender, about 1-1/4 to 1-1/2 hours. Add remaining 1/4 cup water, if needed. Remove rolls from pan drippings and let stand 15 to 20 minutes before slicing with sharp knife. Add mushrooms to pan drippings. Cook until tender, about 5 to 8 minutes. Stir in remaining condensed soup, half and half and paprika. Heat. Serve over sliced meat rolls. Makes 6 to 8 servings.

Cut flank steak to a size that will fit in your skillet. Then, holding the knife horizontally, slit the steak open and lay it flat.

After pounding the slit flank steak to flatten it, sprinkle with salt and pepper. Spread the rice mixture to within an inch of the edges, roll up and tie with string or fasten with skewers.

# Beef & Cheese Crepes

*Crisp salad goes well with this luncheon favorite.*

3/4 cup milk
3 eggs
1/4 teaspoon salt
3/4 cup flour
1 (6-oz.) pkg. UNCLE BEN'S®
   Long Grain & Wild Rice

2-1/2 cups water
1 tablespoon butter or margarine
1 lb. lean ground beef
1 (4-oz.) can sliced mushrooms, drained
Cream of Mushroom Sauce, see below
1 cup shredded process American cheese

*Cream of Mushroom Sauce:*
1/4 cup butter or margarine
2 tablespoons flour
1-1/2 cups milk

1 (10-1/2-oz.) can condensed
   cream of mushroom soup

Combine milk, eggs and salt in a small mixing bowl. Beat slightly. Add flour. Beat until smooth. Cover and refrigerate 1 hour. Cook contents of rice and seasoning packets with water and butter or margarine according to package directions. Cook ground beef until crumbly; drain. Add cooked rice, dill weed and mushrooms. Mix well. Preheat oven to 350°F (177°C). Lightly butter a 6-inch skillet. Heat the skillet on medium heat. Pour 2 tablespoons of crepe batter into skillet. Rotate skillet quickly to spread batter evenly. Cook until lightly browned. Turn. Brown lightly on other side. Turn out; keep warm. Fill each crepe with 1/3 cup rice-beef mixture. Roll up. Place on a large heatproof platter or 13-1/2" x 8-1/2" baking dish. Use remaining rice-beef mixture for sauce. Pour Cream of Mushroom Sauce over crepes. Sprinkle with shredded cheese. Bake until cheese is melted, 15 to 20 minutes. Makes 6 servings (2 crepes per serving).

**Cream of Mushroom Sauce:**

Melt butter or margarine; stir in flour, milk and soup. Cook until thickened, stirring constantly. Stir in remaining rice-beef mixture.

# Stuffed Cabbage

*Cheese and easy cream sauce add pizzazz to rice and vegetables.*

1 (6-oz.) pkg. UNCLE BEN'S®
   Long Grain & Wild Rice
2-1/2 cups water
1 tablespoon butter or margarine
6 cups water
1 large head cabbage
2 tablespoons butter or margarine
1/2 cup chopped celery

1/4 cup chopped onion
1/4 cup chopped cooked carrot
1 (7-oz.) can whole-kernel corn, drained
1 (4-oz.) can mushroom pieces, drained
2 cups shredded Cheddar cheese
1 (10-1/2-oz.) can condensed
   cream-of-mushroom soup
1/4 cup milk

Preheat oven to 350°F (177°C). Lightly butter or oil a 13-1/2" x 8-1/2" baking dish. Cook contents of rice and seasoning packets with water and 1 tablespoon butter or margarine according to package directions. In a large saucepan, bring 6 cups water to boiling. Add cabbage. Simmer until leaves are pliable, about 3 minutes. Drain. Remove outer cabbage leaves (about 24 leaves). Cut out hard center rib at bottom of each leaf. Melt 2 tablespoons butter or margarine in a medium skillet. Add celery, onion, carrot, corn and mushroom pieces. Cook, stirring constantly, until celery and onion are tender, not brown. Stir vegetable mixture and cheese into cooked rice. Place 2 to 4 tablespoons of rice mixture on each cabbage leaf, depending on size of leaf. Roll up, tucking sides in during rolling. Arrange rolls in prepared baking dish, folded side down. Cover with aluminum foil, crimping it tightly to edges of dish. Bake 25 minutes. Combine soup and milk in a medium saucepan. Heat and serve with cabbage rolls. Makes 6 servings.

# Crabmeat Enchiladas

*Splurge on the crabmeat and add as much as you want.*

1 cup UNCLE BEN'S® CONVERTED®
   Brand Rice
2-1/2 cups water
1 teaspoon salt
1 tablespoon butter or margarine
1 or 2 (6-oz.) pkgs. frozen crabmeat,
   thawed and diced
1/4 cup chopped green onion

1 cup shredded Monterey Jack cheese (1/4 lb.)
2 (10-oz.) cans enchilada sauce
1/3 cup vegetable oil, if needed
16 uncooked corn tortillas
1 cup shredded Monterey Jack cheese (1/4 lb.)
1 cup dairy sour cream
Pitted ripe olives, quartered, for garnish

Preheat oven to 350°F (177°C). Cook rice with water, salt and butter or margarine according to package directions. Stir crabmeat, onion, 1 cup cheese and 3 tablespoons of the enchilada sauce into cooked rice. If the tortillas are not soft, heat oil in a small skillet. Heat tortillas in oil, one at a time, until soft. Drain on paper towels. If tortillas are already soft, they need not be softened in oil. Spread each tortilla down center with about 1/4 cup rice mixture. Roll up. Arrange in 13-1/2" x 8-1/2" baking dish. Pour remaining enchilada sauce over tortillas. Cover with aluminum foil, crimping it tightly to edges of dish. Bake 25 minutes. Uncover. Sprinkle with 1 cup cheese. Return to oven until thoroughly heated and cheese melts, 5 to 10 minutes. Top with sour cream. Garnish with olives. Make 8 servings.

# Cranberried Duck With Wild Rice Stuffing

*Roast duck glazed with a rosy cranberry-honey sauce.*

1 (5-lb.) ready-to-cook duck or duckling
1 (6-oz.) pkg. UNCLE BEN'S®
   Long Grain & Wild Rice

2-1/2 cups water
1 tablespoon butter or margarine
About 1/2 cup Cranberry-Honey Sauce, see below

*Cranberry-Honey Sauce:*
1/4 cup sieved cranberry sauce
1 tablespoon honey

1/2 teaspoon bottled brown gravy sauce

Cook duck neck and giblets in lightly salted water and cover until tender, about 1 hour. Add liver last 20 minutes of cooking time. Drain off liquid; reserve for gravy if desired. Dice meat and giblets. Preheat oven to 325°F (163°C). Cook contents of rice and seasoning packets with water and butter or margarine according to package directions. Combine rice with giblets and use to stuff duck lightly. Truss duck or during roasting protect vent opening with a piece of aluminum foil. Place on rack in shallow pan and roast for 1-1/2 hours. Brush Cranberry-Honey Sauce over duck. Continue baking duck until richly browned and glazed, about 1/2 hour longer. Just before serving, brush again with Cranberry-Honey Sauce. Makes 4 servings.

**Cranberry-Honey Sauce:**
Combine cranberry sauce with honey and bottled brown gravy sauce. Makes about 1/2 cup.

# Ham & Rice Stuffed Tomatoes

*Highly seasoned, buttery stuffing in garden-fresh tomatoes.*

2 cups UNCLE BEN'S® QUICK™
   Brand Rice
1-2/3 cups water
1/2 teaspoon salt
1 tablespoon butter or margarine
6 medium, firm ripe tomatoes
2 tablespoons butter or margarine
1/2 cup chopped green pepper
1/4 cup chopped onion
1 clove garlic, minced

1 lb. ground cooked ham
2 eggs, slightly beaten
1/2 cup half and half
1/4 cup chopped parsley
1 teaspoon turmeric
1 teaspoon salt
1/4 teaspoon pepper
1/4 cup fine dry bread crumbs
3 tablespoons butter or margarine

Preheat oven to 425°F (218°C). Lightly butter or oil a 13-1/2" x 8-1/2" baking dish. Cook rice with water, 1/2 teaspoon salt and 1 tablespoon butter or margarine according to package directions. Wash and core tomatoes and cut in half crosswise. Remove a small portion of center to make stuffing easy. In a small saucepan, melt 2 tablespoons butter or margarine. Add green pepper, onion and garlic. Cook until onion is tender, not brown. Combine cooked rice, ham, eggs, half and half, parsley, turmeric, 1 teaspoon salt, pepper and onion mixture. Make rounded, smooth mounds with about 1/3 cup of rice mixture on each tomato half. Sprinkle with an equal amount of bread crumbs. Arrange in buttered or oiled baking dish. Melt 3 tablespoons butter or margarine. Pour over tomato halves. Bake until heated through, about 30 minutes. Makes 6 servings.

# Mediterranean Ham Buffet

*Chill overnight for a heartier flavor.*

2-1/2 cups water
2 chicken-bouillon cubes, crushed
1 teaspoon instant minced onion
1/2 teaspoon salt
1/2 teaspoon garlic salt
1/2 teaspoon monosodium glutamate,
   if desired
1/2 teaspoon sugar
1/8 teaspoon turmeric
1 cup UNCLE BEN'S® CONVERTED®
   Brand Rice

2 (6-oz.) jars marinated artichoke hearts
1/3 cup mayonnaise
1/4 teaspoon curry powder
2 green onions and tops, chopped
1/2 medium green pepper, chopped
14 pitted black olives, sliced
1 cup diced cooked ham
Crisp salad greens

In a large saucepan, bring water to a boil. Stir in bouillon cubes, onion, salt, garlic salt, monosodium glutamate, if desired, sugar, turmeric and rice. Cover tightly and simmer 20 minutes. Remove from heat. Let stand, covered, until all water is absorbed, about 5 minutes. Cool. Drain artichokes; reserve marinade. Cut artichokes in half. In a large bowl, combine marinade, mayonnaise and curry powder. Fold in cooled rice, green onions, green pepper, black olives, ham and artichokes. Chill 4 hours or overnight. Serve on crisp salad greens. Makes 6 servings.

# Ham Véronique

*Tender ham, fruited rice and a rich, gourmet sauce.*

1 (6-oz.) pkg. UNCLE BEN'S®
   Long Grain & Wild Rice
2-1/2 cups water
1 tablespoon butter or margarine
1-1/2 to 2 lb. fully cooked boned ham,
   cut in 3/8-in. slices
2 tablespoons butter or margarine
3/4 cup half and half

1/4 cup currant jelly
1 tablespoon flour
Pinch of salt
1/2 cup dry white wine
1 cup seedless green grapes
   or 1 (8-1/4-oz.) can
   seedless green grapes
1/3 cup toasted slivered almonds

Cook contents of rice and seasoning packets with water and 1 tablespoon butter or margarine according to package directions. In a large skillet, heat ham slices with 2 tablespoons butter about 5 minutes, turning once. Remove from pan; keep warm. Blend half and half, jelly, flour and salt; add to pan drippings. Cook, stirring constantly, until thickened. Add wine. Heat, stirring until bubbly. Stir grapes and almonds into hot cooked rice; heat. Place ham slices over rice and serve sauce over ham. Makes 6 to 8 servings.

# Oriental Quiche

*Pastry with an unusual crunch.*

1 cup UNCLE BEN'S® CONVERTED®
   Brand Rice
2-1/2 cups water
1 teaspoon salt
1 tablespoon butter or margarine
Pastry dough for 10-in. pie shell
1/4 cup toasted sesame seed
1 cup sliced mushrooms
1/4 cup sliced green onion
2 tablespoons butter or margarine

1 (10-1/2-oz.) can condensed oyster stew
1 (4-1/2-oz.) can shrimp, drained and rinsed
1/2 cup chopped water chestnuts
4 eggs, slightly beaten
1/4 teaspoon salt
1/4 teaspoon ground pepper
1/4 teaspoon mace
1/4 teaspoon hot pepper sauce
Tomato slices or wedges

Preheat oven to 400°F (205°C). Cook rice with water, 1 teaspoon salt and 1 tablespoon butter or margarine according to package directions. Prepare pastry from a mix or use your favorite recipe, adding sesame seed. Roll into a circle, 1/8-inch thick, on a lightly floured surface. Fit into a 10-inch pie plate. Trim and flute a high-standing rim. Cook mushrooms and green onions in 2 tablespoons butter or margarine until mushrooms are tender, not brown. Combine cooked rice, mushroom mixture and remaining ingredients except tomato slices or wedges. Mix. Bake crust 5 minutes. Fill with rice mixture. Return to oven. Bake 10 minutes. Reduce heat to 325°F (163°C). Continue baking until mixture is set, about 30 minutes. Let stand 10 minutes. Garnish top with tomato slices or wedges. Cut in wedges. Makes 6 to 8 servings.

# Quick Skillet Dishes

Here are shortcuts that free you from the kitchen in record time. UNCLE BEN'S® QUICK™ Brand Rice and UNCLE BEN'S® Fast Cooking Long Grain & Wild Rice are the secret ingredients. Gazpacho Skillet, Beef & Rice Stroganoff and In-A-Hurry Pork & Zucchini Rice are nourishing meals you can put on the table in minutes. And they're easy, too. In fact, some of these recipes, like Tuna Supper, are so easy your babysitter won't mind putting them together.

### Quick Southern Meal
* Beef & Rice Stroganoff
  Green Beans with Bacon
  Hot Biscuits
  Peaches with Praline Topping

### Something Different
* Oriental Chicken-Cucumber Sauté
  Broccoli Almondine
  Sliced Beet & Onion Salad
  Pineapple

### A Flavor of Spain
* Gazpacho Skillet
  Peas & Mushrooms
  Mixed Greens, Oil &
  Vinegar Dressing
  Melon

### It's Fast and Delicious
* Quick Ham Dinner
  Sliced Tomato & Cucumber
  Ice Cream, Butterscotch Sauce

### Babysitter Special
* Tuna Supper
  Carrot-Raisin Salad
  Ice Cream, Brownies

### Garden Delight
* In-A-Hurry Pork & Zucchini Rice
  Spinach Salad, Creamy Dressing
  Apples & Cheese

*These recipes are in this section.

# Creole Ham Supper

*Leftover ham turns into a great supper treat.*

2 tablespoons olive oil
4 cups cubed, cooked ham
1/2 cup sliced green onions
1 (28-oz.) can plum tomatoes
Water

1/2 teaspoon basil
4 cups UNCLE BEN'S® QUICK™
   Brand Rice
1/4 cup grated Parmesan cheese

In a large skillet, heat oil. Add ham and onions. Sauté until onions are tender and ham is lightly browned, about 3 minutes. Drain tomatoes; reserve liquid. Measure liquid and add water to make 3 cups. Add liquid, tomatoes and basil to ham. Simmer, uncovered, 5 minutes. Bring to a *vigorous* boil. Stir in rice. Cover. Simmer until all liquid has been absorbed, about 5 minutes. Stir in cheese just before serving. Makes 6 to 8 servings.


# Sausage & Rice

*So easy and delicious.*

1 lb. bulk pork sausage
3 cups UNCLE BEN'S® QUICK™
   Brand Rice
2 cups water

1 (10-3/4-oz.) can condensed
   cream-of-chicken soup
1/2 teaspoon salt
1/2 cup sliced ripe olives

In a large skillet, brown sausage; drain. Stir in rice, water, soup and salt. Bring to a *vigorous* boil. Cover. Simmer about 5 minutes or until rice is tender and mixture is desired consistency. Stir in olives. Makes 4 to 6 servings.


# California Easy-Living Supper

*Casual and delicious.*

1 lb. ground beef
1 medium onion, chopped
1 clove garlic, minced
3 cups UNCLE BEN'S® QUICK™
   Brand Rice
2-1/4 cups water
2-1/2 teaspoons salt

3/4 teaspoon ground cinnamon
1 teaspoon chili powder
2 medium tomatoes, chopped
1/3 cup seedless raisins
1/4 medium head lettuce,
   coarsely chopped
1 tablespoon lemon juice

In a large skillet, brown meat. Pour off drippings. Stir in onion, garlic, rice, water, salt, cinnamon and chili powder. Bring to a boil. Cover. Simmer until liquid is absorbed, about 5 minutes. Stir in tomatoes and raisins; heat thoroughly. Just before serving, stir in lettuce and lemon juice. Makes 6 servings.

# Sweet & Sour Pork

*Follow this with scoops of lemon sherbet and fortune cookies.*

2 tablespoons vegetable oil
1 lb. boneless pork, cut in
   3/4-in. cubes
1 (13-1/4-oz.) can pineapple tidbits
Water
1/4 cup vinegar
1-1/2 teaspoons salt

1/2 teaspoon garlic salt
2 tablespoons sugar
1 cup UNCLE BEN'S® CONVERTED®
   Brand Rice
1 green pepper, cut into small squares
1 tomato, cut into thin wedges

In a large skillet, heat oil. Add pork and brown well; drain. Drain pineapple tidbits; reserve liquid. Add water to liquid to make 2-1/2 cups liquid. Add liquid, vinegar, salt, garlic salt and sugar to pork. Stir. Bring to a boil. Reduce heat and cover. Cook over low heat 20 minutes. Remove cover; stir in rice. Cover and simmer 20 minutes. Remove from heat. Let stand, covered, until all liquid is absorbed and pork is tender, about 5 minutes. Stir in pineapple tidbits, green pepper and tomato wedges. Makes 4 to 6 servings.

Variations:

Substitute cubed ham or cubed uncooked chicken for pork.

Omit browning step and fold in cubed *cooked* chicken, pork or turkey, shrimp or tuna during cooking time for rice. Reduce total cooking time to 25 minutes.

Combine browned pork, pineapple liquid, water, vinegar, salt, garlic salt and sugar. Simmer for 20 minutes. Add rice and simmer another 20 minutes.

After all liquid is absorbed, stir in pineapple, green pepper and tomato wedges.

# Tex-Mex Chili

*Beef, chili and rice blend in an easy skillet dish.*

1 lb. ground beef
4 cups UNCLE BEN'S® QUICK™
    Brand Rice
3 cups water
1 cup chopped onion
1 large green pepper, chopped

1 (1-1/4-oz.) pkg. chili-seasoning mix
1 (1-lb.) can tomatoes, undrained
1 (1-lb.) can kidney beans, drained
1 tablespoon salt
1 cup shredded Cheddar or Monterey
    Jack cheese

In a large skillet, brown meat; drain. Add remaining ingredients except cheese; stir. Bring to a *vigorous* boil. Cover tightly. Simmer about 5 minutes or until desired consistency. Sprinkle with cheese. Makes 8 servings.

# Camper's Rice Fry

*Chinese fried rice—delicious cooked over the campfire.*

2 tablespoons bacon drippings or butter
1 (4-oz.) can sliced mushrooms
1/2 cup sliced green onions, including tops
1/4 cup sliced celery and leaves
1 (4-oz.) pkg. smoked sliced beef,
    coarsely diced

Chicken stock
1 tablespoon soy sauce
2 cups UNCLE BEN'S® QUICK™
    Brand Rice
1 egg, well beaten

In a large skillet, heat bacon drippings or butter. Drain mushrooms; reserve liquid. Add onions, celery and leaves, mushrooms and beef. Sauté 3 minutes. Add enough chicken stock to mushroom liquid to make 1-2/3 cups. Bring to a *vigorous* boil. Add soy sauce and rice. Cover. Simmer until all liquid is absorbed, about 5 minutes. Uncover. Add egg and stir until egg is cooked. Makes 4 servings.

# Quick Taco Skillet

*This is the "in" rice dish.*

1 lb. ground beef
3 cups UNCLE BEN'S® QUICK™
    Brand Rice
1 (1-lb.) can tomato wedges
1 (13-3/4-oz.) can beef broth
1 medium onion, sliced

1-1/2 teaspoons salt
2 teaspoons chili powder
2 cups shredded lettuce
1 cup shredded Cheddar cheese
1 avocado, sliced, for garnish
Taco chips, for garnish

In a large skillet, brown beef; drain. Stir in rice, tomato wedges with liquid, beef broth, onion, salt and chili powder. Bring to a *vigorous* boil. Cover. Simmer until all liquid is absorbed, about 5 minutes. Serve hot, topped with shredded lettuce and cheese. Garnish with avocado slices and taco chips. Makes 4 to 6 servings.

# Stir-Fry Ham & Peaches

*Quick-cooked ham and vegetables in a spicy peach sauce.*

1 cup fresh or frozen peas
1 (1-lb. 13-oz.) can sliced cling peaches
3/4 cup water
3 tablespoons dry sherry
3 tablespoons soy sauce
2 tablespoons honey
2 tablespoons cornstarch
1/4 teaspoon ground ginger

2 tablespoons vegetable oil
1 clove garlic, sliced
1 lb. fully cooked ham, thinly sliced
1/2 cup minced green onion
1 (8-1/2-oz.) can water chestnuts, drained and sliced
2 to 3 cups UNCLE BEN'S® QUICK™ Brand Rice, *cooked*

Thaw peas, if frozen. Drain sliced peaches; reserve 1/2 cup syrup. Combine reserved syrup, water, sherry, soy sauce, honey, cornstarch and ginger. Mix well. In a large skillet, heat oil and garlic over high heat until garlic is brown; remove and discard. Add ham, a few pieces at a time, making sure skillet remains very hot. Cook and stir 1 to 2 minutes. Add peas and green onion. Cook and stir 1 minute. Stir cornstarch mixture and add to ham and vegetables. Cook, stirring constantly, until thickened. Add sliced peaches and water chestnuts. Stir to coat with sauce. Heat thoroughly. Serve immediately over hot cooked rice. Makes 4 to 6 servings.

# Calcutta Casserole

*A real crowd-pleaser—quick and delicious.*

2 tablespoons vegetable oil
1 tablespoon salt
1-1/2 teaspoons ground coriander
1 teaspoon whole black peppercorns
1/2 teaspoon ground allspice
1/2 teaspoon mustard seed
1/2 teaspoon oregano
1/2 teaspoon sugar
1/2 teaspoon turmeric
3 or 4 whole cumin seeds
2 whole cloves

1 stick cinnamon
2 tablespoons chopped blanched almonds
2 carrots, sliced
2 small onions, coarsely chopped
1/2 cup water
2 cups UNCLE BEN'S® CONVERTED® Brand Rice
3-1/2 cups water
2-1/2 cups cauliflowerets
1/2 cup frozen peas, thawed
1/4 cup seedless raisins

Heat oil in a 3-quart saucepan. Add salt, coriander, peppercorns, allspice, mustard seed, oregano, sugar, turmeric, cumin seeds, cloves and cinnamon. Mix well. Add almonds, carrots and onions; stir to coat vegetables with spices. Add 1/2 cup water and cover. Simmer gently 5 minutes. Add rice, 3-1/2 cups water, cauliflowerets, peas and raisins. Mix and cover. Simmer until water is absorbed, about 20 minutes. Remove cinnamon stick. Makes 10 servings.

# In-a-Hurry Pork & Zucchini Rice

*A hearty, quick supper dish.*

3 cups UNCLE BEN'S® QUICK™
  Brand Rice
2-1/3 cups water
1 tablespoon butter or margarine
2 teaspoons salt
3 medium zucchini, diced
2 tablespoons flour
1 teaspoon salt
1 lb. boneless pork, cut into thin strips

2 tablespoons vegetable oil
1 medium onion, chopped
1 clove garlic, minced
1 (10-1/2-oz.) can chicken gravy
2 tablespoons sherry
1/2 teaspoon sage
1 (2-oz.) jar sliced pimiento,
  drained

In a large saucepan, combine rice, water, butter or margarine and 2 teaspoons salt. Stir. Bring to a *vigorous* boil. Reduce heat and cover. Simmer until liquid is absorbed, about 5 minutes. Stir in zucchini. Cover and heat through, about 5 minutes. Combine flour and 1 teaspoon salt. Dredge pork strips in flour mixture. In a large skillet, heat oil over moderately high heat. Add meat. Stir and brown well, about 5 minutes. Add onion and garlic and stir. Cook until onion is tender, about 5 minutes. Stir in gravy, sherry, sage and pimiento. Heat through. Serve over rice. Makes 4 to 6 servings.


# Quick Ham Dinner

*Plump, juicy raisins soaked in orange juice flavor this unusual dinner.*

1 (6-oz.) pkg. UNCLE BEN'S®
  Long Grain & Wild Rice
1/4 cup sherry
2-1/4 cups water
1 tablespoon butter or margarine
1/2 cup cup raisins
1/2 cup orange juice
1 (13-1/4-oz.) can pineapple tidbits,
  packed in syrup

1/4 cup sugar
1 tablespoon cornstarch
2 teaspoons butter or margarine
6 slices cooked ham
  (about 1/4-in. thick)
1/2 cup chopped pecans
2 green onions, sliced

Cook contents of rice and seasoning packets with sherry, water and 1 tablespoon butter or margarine according to package directions. Soak raisins in orange juice. Drain pineapple tidbits; reserve syrup. In a small saucepan, combine pineapple syrup, raisin and orange-juice mixture, sugar and cornstarch. Mix well. Cook over low heat until thickened, stirring constantly. Stir pineapple tidbits into sauce and heat. In a large skillet, melt 2 teaspoons butter or margarine. Add ham. Brown 4 to 5 minutes, turning once. Stir pecans and green onions into cooked rice. Serve ham and sauce with rice. Makes 4 to 6 servings.

# Gazpacho Skillet

*Classic Spanish-soup flavors in a quick and easy skillet.*

1 lb. ground beef
1 cup UNCLE BEN'S® CONVERTED®
  Brand Rice
1 medium onion, sliced
1 clove garlic, minced
2-1/2 cups tomato juice
1/4 cup red wine vinegar

2-1/2 to 3 teaspoons salt
1/4 teaspoon pepper
1/4 teaspoon hot pepper sauce
1 medium green pepper, chopped
1 medium tomato, chopped
1 medium cucumber,
  peeled and chopped

In a large skillet, brown beef; drain. Add rice, onion, garlic, tomato juice, vinegar, salt, pepper and hot pepper sauce. Stir. Bring to a boil. Reduce heat and cover tightly. Simmer 20 minutes. Remove from heat. Stir green pepper, tomato and cucumber into cooked rice. Cover and heat about 5 minutes. Makes 4 to 6 servings.

# Uncle Ben's Ragoût

*Inspired by the classic French stew.*

1 lb. ground beef
1 (1-lb.) can tomatoes
Water
1 (1-3/8-oz.) envelope dry onion-soup mix
1 cup UNCLE BEN'S® CONVERTED®
  Brand Rice

1/2 teaspoon garlic salt
1/2 cup sliced stuffed green olives
1/4 cup grated Cheddar cheese

In a large skillet, brown beef; drain. Drain and cut up tomatoes; reserve juice. Add water to juice to make 2-1/2 cups liquid. Add tomatoes, liquid, onion-soup mix, rice and garlic salt to beef. Stir. Bring to a boil and cover tightly. Simmer 20 minutes. Remove from heat. Let stand, covered, until all liquid is absorbed, about 5 minutes. Before serving, sprinkle with olives and cheese. Cover skillet until cheese melts. Makes 4 to 6 servings.

**Variation:**
Omit ground beef and browning step. Substitute cubed cooked roast beef, pot roast or other cooked beef.

Gazpacho Skillet

# Chinese Pepper Beef

*Youngsters enjoy this Chinese-style dish.*

1 lb. ground beef
Water
1 (13-3/4-oz.) can beef broth
1 tablespoon cornstarch
3 cups UNCLE BEN'S® QUICK™
   Brand Rice
1 medium onion, sliced

1 tablespoon soy sauce
1 teaspoon salt
1/2 teaspoon ground ginger
1 green pepper, cut in strips
12 cherry tomatoes,
   cut in halves

In a large skillet, brown beef; drain. Add water to beef broth to make 3 cups liquid. Blend in cornstarch. Add liquid with cornstarch, rice, onion, soy sauce, salt and ginger to beef. Stir. Bring to a boil. Cover. Simmer until all liquid is absorbed, about 5 minutes. Stir in green pepper and tomatoes. Heat through. Makes 4 to 6 servings.

**Variation:**
For extra crunch, fold in Chinese noodles just before serving.

# Tuna Supper

*The economical standby does it again.*

3 cups UNCLE BEN'S® QUICK™
   Brand Rice
2-1/4 cups water
1 (10-1/2-oz.) can condensed
   cream-of-mushroom soup
1/2 cup chopped onion

1 (10-oz.) pkg. frozen mixed vegetables,
   thawed
1 (6-1/2-oz.) can tuna,
   drained and flaked
1-1/2 teaspoons salt

In a large, heavy skillet combine all ingredients; stir. Bring to a boil. Cover. Simmer about 5 minutes or until vegetables are tender and mixture is desired consistency. Makes 4 to 6 servings.

**Varation:**
Stir in 1 (2-oz.) jar sliced pimiento, drained, before serving.

# Mediterranean Beef & Artichokes

*No one will know you did it in half an hour.*

1 (1-lb.) can tomato wedges
Water
1 (6-oz.) jar marinated artichoke hearts
1-1/2 lbs. beef round steak,
   cut in thin strips

1-1/2 teaspoon salt
3 cups UNCLE BEN'S® QUICK™
   Brand Rice
3 green onions, sliced
Sliced ripe olives, if desired

Drain tomato wedges; reserve juice. Add water to juice to make 2-1/3 cups liquid. Drain artichoke hearts, reserve marinade. Cut artichokes in half. Heat marinade in skillet. Add meat and brown, turning as needed. Add tomato wedges, liquid and salt; stir. Bring to a boil. Stir in rice. Reduce heat and cover. Simmer over low heat until liquid is absorbed, about 5 minutes. Add artichoke hearts. Cover and heat. Sprinkle with green onion and sliced ripe olives, if desired. Makes 6 servings.

# Quick Paella

*Flamenco dancers' favorite.*

1 (1-lb.) can tomatoes
Water
1 cup UNCLE BEN'S® CONVERTED®
   Brand Rice
1 medium onion, chopped
1 clove garlic, minced
2 tablespoons olive oil

1 chicken-bouillon cube, crushed
2-1/2 teaspoons salt
Pinch of powdered saffron
1-1/2 cups diced cooked chicken
1 (4-1/2-oz.) can small shrimp,
   drained and rinsed
1 cup frozen peas, thawed

Drain tomatoes; reserve juice. Chop tomatoes in large pieces. Add water to juice to make 2-1/2 cups liquid. In a large skillet, cook rice, onion and garlic in olive oil until golden. Add tomato liquid, chicken-bouillon cube, salt and saffron; stir. Bring to a boil. Cover tightly. Simmer 20 minutes. Remove from heat. Stir chicken, shrimp, peas and tomato pieces into rice. Cover. Heat about 5 minutes. Makes 4 to 6 servings.

# Stir-Fry Chicken & Pea Pods

*Pungent and crunchy chicken 'n rice.*

3 cups UNCLE BEN'S® QUICK™
  Brand Rice
2-1/3 cups water
3/4 teaspoon salt
1-1/2 tablespoons butter or margarine
1 cup water
1 chicken-bouillon cube, crumbled
2 tablespoons soy sauce
1 tablespoon cornstarch
1 teaspoon garlic salt

1/4 teaspoon tarragon
2 tablespoons vegetable oil
2 lbs. chicken breasts, skinned, boned
  and cut in 3/4-in. cubes
1 tablespoon vegetable oil
1 (6-oz.) pkg. frozen Chinese pea pods,
  thawed
1 (8-oz.) can water chestnuts,
  drained and sliced
2 green onions, sliced

Cook rice with 2-1/3 cups water, salt and butter or margarine according to package directions. In a small bowl, combine 1 cup water, bouillon cube, soy sauce, cornstarch, garlic salt and tarragon. Stir until free of lumps. In a large skillet, heat 2 tablespoons of oil. Add chicken. Cook and stir over high heat until meat turns white, 2 to 3 minutes. Remove chicken from skillet and keep warm. Add 1 tablespoon oil to wok or skillet. Add pea pods. Cook and stir just until tender, about 2 minutes. Add water chestnuts and cornstarch mixture. Cook and stir until sauce is thickened and clear. Add chicken. Stir green onion into hot cooked rice. Makes 4 to 6 servings.

**Stir cornstarch mixture until it's free of lumps. In a wok or skillet, cook chicken over high heat until it turns white. Remove chicken from the pan.**

**In the same wok or skillet cook the pea pods. Add water chestnuts and cornstarch mixture. Cook, stirring until sauce thickens and becomes clear. Add the cooked chicken.**

# Veal & Orange Skillet Dinner

*Veal and vegetables in a family-pleasing dish.*

2 tablespoons butter or margarine
6 medium carrots, thinly sliced
  (about 1-1/2 cups)
1 medium onion, chopped
1 tablespoon butter or margarine
1-1/2 lbs. veal steak, cut in thin strips
3 cups UNCLE BEN'S® QUICK™
  Brand Rice

1-1/2 teaspoons garlic salt
1 teaspoon sugar
Water
1 (13-3/4-oz.) can chicken broth
1 medium orange
2 tablespoons chopped parsley

In a large skillet, melt 2 tablespoons butter or margarine. Add carrots and onion. Cook over very low heat until carrots are almost tender, about 10 minutes. Remove from skillet. Add 1 tablespoon butter or margarine. Add veal and brown, turning as needed. Add rice, garlic salt, sugar, carrots and onion. Add water to chicken broth to make 2-1/3 cups liquid. Add liquid to rice-veal mixture and stir. Bring to a boil. Reduce heat and cover. Simmer over low heat until liquid is absorbed, about 5 minutes. Peel and section orange. Add orange sections to rice mixture; heat. Sprinkle with parsley. Makes 6 servings.

# Beef & Rice Stroganoff

*This basic recipe gives you room for your own variations.*

1 lb. ground beef
1 cup UNCLE BEN'S® CONVERTED®
  Brand Rice
2-1/4 cups water
1 teaspoon salt

1 teaspoon garlic salt
1 cup sliced onion
1 (10-1/2-oz.) can condensed cream-of-
  mushroom soup
1/3 cup catsup

In a large skillet, brown beef; drain. Stir in rice, water, salt, garlic salt, onion, soup and catsup. Bring to a boil. Cover tightly and simmer 20 minutes. Remove from heat. Let stand covered until most of liquid is absorbed, about 5 minutes. Makes 4 to 6 servings.

**Variations:**

Omit ground beef and browning step. Substitute cubed cooked roast beef, beef pot roast or other cooked beef.

Substitute 1 (10-1/2-oz.) can condensed cream-of-chicken soup plus 1 small can mushrooms, drained, for condensed cream-of-mushroom soup.

# Swiss-Sausage Rice

*Supper with a European touch.*

2 tablespoons butter or margarine
3 medium onions, sliced
1 clove garlic, minced
2 tablespoons butter or margarine
3 cups UNCLE BEN'S® QUICK™
   Brand Rice
1 teaspoon salt

1 (13-3/4-oz.) can chicken broth
Water
1 (12-oz.) pkg. smoked sausage links,
   cut in thirds
1/2 cup shredded Swiss cheese
2 tablespoons chopped parsley

In a large skillet, melt butter or margarine. Add onions and garlic. Cook very slowly until tender, but not brown. Add rice and salt. Add water to chicken broth to make 2-1/3 cups liquid. Add liquid to rice and stir. Arrange sausage links on top of rice. Bring to a boil. Reduce heat and cover. Simmer over low heat until liquid is absorbed, about 5 minutes. Sprinkle with cheese. Cover and allow cheese to soften. Sprinkle with parsley. Makes 4 to 6 servings.

# Oriental Chicken-Cucumber Sauté

*Try this one in your wok.*

2 cups UNCLE BEN'S® QUICK™
   Brand Rice
1-2/3 cups water
1/2 teaspoon salt
1 tablespoon butter or margarine
1 (4-oz.) can sliced mushrooms
Water
1 chicken-bouillon cube, crumbled
1 tablespoon cornstarch

1 teaspoon garlic salt
2 tablespoons vegetable oil
1-1/2 lbs. chicken breasts or
   chicken breasts and thighs, boned,
   skinned and cut in strips
1 tablespoon vegetable oil
1 large cucumber, peeled and sliced
1 (2-oz.) jar sliced pimiento, drained
2 teaspoons soy sauce

Cook rice with water, salt and butter or margarine according to package directions. Drain mushrooms; reserve liquid. Add water to liquid to make 1 cup. In a small saucepan, combine liquid, bouillon cube, cornstarch and garlic salt. Stir until free of lumps. Heat 2 tablespoons of the oil in a large skillet. Add chicken. Cook and stir over high heat until meat turns white, 2 to 3 minutes. Remove chicken from skillet and keep warm. Add 1 tablespoon oil to skillet. Add cucumber and mushrooms. Cook and stir just until cucumber is heated, about 1 minute. Add cornstarch mixture. Cook and stir until sauce is thickened and clear. Add chicken and pimiento. Just before serving, stir in soy sauce. Serve over hot cooked rice. Makes 4 servings.

# Make Ahead

It's the dream of every host and hostess to have plenty of time to have everything party-perfect before the guests arrive. With these recipes and menu ideas, you can have all the time you need. Prepare the meal for your dinner party the night before or first thing in the morning and put it in the refrigerator. That evening, an hour or so before serving, pop it in the oven while you set the table. Try Beef Paprikash for a great family party. If company's coming, serve sophisticated Coq au Bourguignon. With UNCLE BEN'S® Make-Ahead recipes you'll have a delicious dinner with almost no clutter and confusion in the kitchen, leaving you free to enjoy your guests.

*Chicken Never Tasted So Great!*
* Coq Au Bourguignon
  Broiled Tomato Halves
  Mixed Greens,
  Vinaigarette Dressing
  French Pastry

*Stay For Lunch*
* Ham a la King with Pecan Rice
  Broccoli Polonaise
  Cheese-Topped Biscuits
  Broiled Grapefruit Halves

*Dad's Favorite*
* Beef Paprikash
  Glazed Carrots
  Sweet & Sour Cabbage Salad
  Crescent Rolls
  Apple-Nut Cake

*Saturday Night Special*
* Onion-Fried Chicken & Wild Rice
  Zucchini & Yellow Squash
  Cucumber-Tomato Salad
  Cheesecake

*Hurry-Up Dinner*
  Broiled Hamburger Patties
* Broccoli Bake With Wild Rice
  Mixed Greens, Sesame Dressing
  Plum Cake

*Down-Home Eating*
* Spanish Pork and Rice
  Creamed Spinach
  Carrot & Celery Sticks
  Applesauce-Topped Gingerbread

*These recipes are in this section.*

# Coq au Bourguignon

*A romantic dinner for connoisseurs.*

4 large chicken breasts
4 slices bacon, diced
1 cup boiling water
12 tiny white onions
2 tablespoons butter or margarine
1/3 cup brandy
3 cups Burgundy
1 cup beef stock
Salt and pepper to taste
2 cloves garlic, minced

1 Bouquet Garni, see below
1 lb. small mushroom caps
1 cup UNCLE BEN'S® CONVERTED®
   Brand Rice
2-1/2 cups water
1 teaspoon salt
1 tablespoon butter or margarine
2 tablespoons butter or margarine
1 tablespoon flour

*Bouquet Garni:*
3 sprigs parsley
1 sprig thyme

1 bay leaf

Skin and bone chicken. Cut into bite-size pieces. In a small bowl, cover bacon with boiling water and let stand 5 minutes. Pour off liquid. In a large skillet, melt 2 tablespoons butter or margarine. Add onions and bacon; brown. Remove onions and bacon. Add chicken; brown. In a small saucepan, heat brandy so it will flame easily. Pour over chicken and ignite. Stir gently until flame dies. Add Burgundy, beef stock, salt and pepper to taste, garlic and Bouquet Garni. Bring to a simmer. Add onions, bacon and mushroom caps. Cover. Simmer until chicken is tender, about 45 minutes. Remove Bouquet Garni and refrigerate until ready to use.

Before serving, cook rice with water, 1 teaspoon salt and 1 tablespoon butter or margarine according to package directions; keep warm. Remove congealed fat on surface of chicken. Reheat fat in small pan. When bubbling, blend 2 tablespoons butter or margarine with flour. Stir into chicken. Cook, stirring constantly, until thickened. Serve chicken over hot cooked rice. Makes 4 to 6 servings.

**Bouquet Garni**
Combine parsley, thyme and bay leaf in the center of a 6-inch square of cheesecloth. Gather the corners and edges of the square together and tie tightly.

# Provencale Beef

*Cheese, olives and tomatoes add color to this hearty meal.*

2 tablespoons olive oil
2 lbs. beef chunk or round, cut in
   1-in. chunks
2 medium onions, chopped
1 clove garlic, minced
1 (13-3/4-oz.) can beef broth
1/2 cup dry white vermouth
1 teaspoon salt

1/2 teaspoon leaf thyme
1 bay leaf
1 cup UNCLE BEN'S® CONVERTED®
   Brand Rice
3 tomatoes, chopped
1/2 cup pitted small ripe olives
1 teaspoon salt
1 cup shredded Swiss cheese

Preheat oven to 325°F (163°C). In a Dutch oven or large iron skillet, heat olive oil. Add beef and brown, turning as necessary to brown evenly. Add onions and garlic. Cook until onion is tender, not brown. Add 1 cup beef broth and vermouth. Bring to a boil. Add 1 teaspoon of salt, thyme and bay leaf. Stir. Cover and bake for 1-1/2 hours. Refrigerate until ready to use.

Before serving, stir in rice, remaining beef broth, 2 tomatoes and 1 teaspoon salt. Bring to boil on top of range. Cover. Continue cooking until liquid is absorbed and meat is tender, about 30 minutes. Stir in remaining tomato and olives. Heat through. Sprinkle with cheese. Makes 6 servings.

# Onion-Fried Chicken and Wild Rice

*Canned onion rings make a fabulous crisp coating.*

1 (3-oz.) can French-fried onions
3 lbs. chicken pieces
1 teaspoon salt
1 (6-oz.) pkg. UNCLE BEN'S®
   Long Grain & Wild Rice

2-1/2 cups water
1 tablespoon butter or margarine
1 cup sliced celery

Crush French-fried onions with fingers to make coarse crumbs. Coat chicken pieces with onion crumbs. Arrange in shallow 15" x 10" x 1" baking pan. Sprinkle with salt. Cover with aluminum foil, crimping it to edges of pan. Refrigerate until ready to use.

Before serving, bake at 350°F (177°C) for 55 to 60 minutes. Uncover. Continue baking until onion crumbs are browned and chicken is tender, about 20 minutes. Cook contents of rice and seasoning packets with water and butter or margarine according to package directions. Stir celery into hot cooked rice. Serve chicken on rice. Makes 6 servings.

# Coulibiac

*Fill this light and crisp pastry with a different meat or fish every time you make it.*

1 tablespoon butter or margarine
1/2 lb. fresh mushrooms, sliced
2 tablespoons butter or margarine
Water
1 (13-3/4-oz.) can chicken broth
1 cup UNCLE BEN'S® CONVERTED®
   Brand Rice
1 teaspoon salt
2 (11-oz.) pkgs. pie-crust mix

2 cups flaked, cooked or canned salmon or
   cooked diced chicken, beef or veal
1/4 cup chopped parsley
8 finely sliced green onions
Salt and pepper to taste
1 egg, slightly beaten
1 tablespoon milk
Dairy sour cream or melted butter

Butter a large cookie sheet with 1 tablespoon butter or margarine. In a large skillet, sauté the mushrooms in 2 tablespoons butter or margarine. Add water to chicken broth to make 2-1/2 cups liquid. Add to mushrooms. Bring to boil. Stir in rice and salt. Cover tightly and simmer 20 minutes. Remove from heat. Let stand, covered, until all liquid is absorbed, about 5 minutes. Spoon the rice into a large bowl. Cover and refrigerate until chilled. Prepare dough according to package directions; chill. Cut the chilled dough in half and roll one piece into a 7" x 15" rectangle. Place it on the buttered cookie sheet. Combine chilled rice with the salmon, chicken or meat, parsley, onions, salt and pepper to taste. Spoon the rice filling into the center of the pastry, leaving a border of pastry about 1-1/2 inches wide. Mix together the beaten egg and milk. Brush the pastry border with the egg-milk mixture. Roll the second half of the pastry into a 9" x 17" rectangle. Place it on top of the filling so that the borders of both pieces of pastry meet evenly. Gently press the border around the entire loaf and brush again with the egg-milk mixture. Without stretching the pastry, roll up the border toward the filling, creating a rope effect. With the back of a knife, make 1/8-inch cuts 1 inch apart into the rope. Refrigerate until ready to use.

Before serving, preheat the oven to 400°F (205°C). Make 2 to 3 diagonal slits in the top of the pastry and brush entire surface with the egg-milk mixture. Bake until golden brown, about 50 to 60 minutes. Serve with dairy sour cream or melted butter. Makes 6 servings.

# Curried Chicken & Wild Rice Bake

*Raisins add flavor and texture to this exotic casserole.*

3 large chicken breasts, halved
1 teaspoon salt
1/2 teaspoon curry powder
1/4 teaspoon paprika
1/4 cup butter or margarine, melted

1 (6-oz.) pkg. UNCLE BEN'S®
   Long Grain & Wild Rice
1 tablespoon butter or margarine
1/2 cup seedless raisins
2-1/2 cups boiling water

Preheat oven to 350°F (177°C). Arrange chicken pieces, skin side down, in a shallow 2-quart baking dish. Sprinkle with half the salt, curry powder, and paprika. Drizzle with half the melted butter or margarine. Bake, uncovered, 30 minutes. Turn chicken. Sprinkle with remaining salt, curry powder and paprika and drizzle with remaining melted butter or margarine. Return to oven. Bake until chicken is tender, about 45 minutes. Cover and refrigerate until ready to serve.

Before serving, preheat oven to 350°F (177°C). Place contents of rice and seasoning packets, 1 tablespoon butter or margarine and raisins in a 1-quart casserole. Add boiling water. Stir and cover. Bake in oven with chicken about 40 minutes or until all liquid is absorbed. Serve chicken on top of rice. Makes 6 servings.

# Savory Chicken Kiev With Pecan Wild Rice

*A memorable meal.*

1 (6-oz.) pkg. UNCLE BEN'S®
   Long Grain & Wild Rice
1/2 cup butter or margarine
3 large chicken breasts
   (3/4 to 1 lb. each)
1/4 cup flour for coating
1 egg, beaten

2/3 cup fine corn flakes or bread crumbs
2-1/2 cups water
1 tablespoon butter or margarine
1 teaspoon salt
1/3 cup chopped pecans
1 tablespoon chopped parsley

In advance, cream contents of rice-seasoning packet and 1/2 cup butter or margarine together. Shape into a 4-inch-long roll. Chill. Cut in half crosswise and then lengthwise into 3 equal pieces. Slice chicken breasts in half; skin and bone them carefully. Place each piece of chicken between sheets of waxed paper; pound with side of meat mallet or rolling pin until very thin. Place a piece of the seasoned butter on each piece of chicken. Fold sides of chicken pieces over butter to seal completely and roll up. Fasten with small metal or wooden skewers. Roll in flour. Dip in egg and roll in corn flakes or bread crumbs to coat evenly. Refrigerate at least 1 hour before cooking.

Before serving, preheat oven to 450°F (233°C). Butter a shallow baking pan. In a medium sauce-pan, combine rice, water, 1 tablespoon butter or margarine and salt. Bring to a boil. Cover tightly. Cook over low heat until all water is absorbed, about 25 minutes. Arrange chilled rolls in buttered baking pan. Bake until chicken is tender, about 18 to 20 minutes. Stir pecans and parsley into rice. Serve chicken rolls on rice. Makes 6 servings.

# Beef Paprikash

*A Hungarian blend of spicy flavors.*

1-1/2 lbs. beef
3 tablespoons flour
Salt, pepper
3 tablespoons vegetable oil
1 onion, diced
1 tablespoon paprika
1 (10-oz.) can tomatoes
1 (4-oz.) can mushrooms

1 cup dairy sour cream
Salt and pepper to taste
2 cups UNCLE BEN'S® QUICK™
  Brand Rice
1-2/3 cups water
2 beef-bouillon cubes, crushed
1 tablespoon chopped parsley

Cut beef into 1-1/2-inch cubes. Dredge in flour seasoned with salt and pepper. In a large skillet heat oil. Add beef cubes. Brown on all sides. Add onion and brown lightly. Add paprika and remaining seasoned flour. Stir until smooth. Add liquid from tomatoes. Reserve tomatoes. Cook, stirring constantly, until smooth. Add mushrooms with liquid. Cover. Simmer 1 hour or until meat is tender. Refrigerate until ready to use.

Before serving, stir in sour cream and heat without boiling. Add salt and pepper to taste. Combine rice, water and bouillon cubes. Bring to a *vigorous* boil. Cover and simmer until all liquid is absorbed, about 5 minutes. Dice reserved tomatoes. Combine with parsley and rice. Toss to mix well. Shape rice-tomato mixture on serving platter. Spoon Beef Paprikash over rice. Makes 4 to 6 servings.

# Ham a la King With Pecan Rice

*Pecans and mushrooms give party airs to leftover ham.*

1/4 cup butter
1 medium green pepper, seeded and
  cut into 2-in. strips
1 cup sliced fresh mushrooms
1/4 cup flour
1/2 teaspoon salt
1/4 cup dry sherry
3/4 cup half and half
1 (2-oz.) jar sliced pimiento, drained

3 cups cubed ham (1/3-inch)
1 (6-oz.) pkg. UNCLE BEN'S®
  Long Grain & Wild Rice
2-1/2 cups water
1 tablespoon butter or margarine
1 tablespoon butter or margarine
1/2 cup pecans, halved or coarsely
  chopped
1/4 cup chopped parsley

Melt 1/4 cup butter or margarine in a large saucepan. Add green pepper and mushrooms. Cook, stirring constantly, for 3 minutes. Blend in flour and 1/2 teaspoon salt. Gradually stir in sherry and half and half. Cook, stirring constantly, until sauce is thickened and smooth. Blend in pimiento and ham. Refrigerate until ready to use.

Before serving, cook contents of rice and seasoning packets with water and 1 tablespoon butter or margarine according to package directions. Melt 1 tablespoon butter or margarine in a small skillet. Add pecans and sauté, stirring constantly, until pecans are crisp and lightly browned. Add pecans and chopped parsley to cooked rice; mix gently. Heat ham mixture. To serve, spoon ham mixture over pecan rice. Makes 6 servings.

# Broccoli Bake With Wild Rice

*Green vegetables with taste appeal*

1 (6-oz.) pkg. UNCLE BEN'S®
   Long Grain & Wild Rice
2-1/2 cups water
1 tablespoon butter or margarine
1 cup sliced celery
2 (10-oz.) pkgs. frozen broccoli spears,
   cooked and drained
3 tablespoons butter or margarine

3 tablespoons flour
1/4 teaspoon salt
2 cups milk
1 chicken-bouillon cube, crushed
1/4 cup grated Parmesan cheese
1 tablespoon lemon juice
1/4 cup grated Parmesan cheese

Cook contents of rice and seasoning packets with water and 1 tablespoon butter or margarine according to package directions. Uncover, stir celery into cooked rice. Spoon rice in an even layer into a shallow 2-quart casserole. Arrange broccoli spears on top. In a medium saucepan, melt 3 tablespoons butter or margarine. Stir in flour and salt. Add milk and bouillon cube. Cook, stirring constantly, until smooth and thickened. Stir in 1/4 cup of Parmesan cheese and the lemon juice. Pour over broccoli. Sprinkle with remaining 1/4 cup of cheese. Cover and refrigerate until ready to use.

Before serving bake at 375°F (191°C) until hot and bubbly, about 35 to 40 minutes. Makes 6 to 8 servings.

**Variation:**
Substitute 2 (10-oz.) pkgs. asparagus spears for the broccoli.

**Spoon an even layer of rice-celery mixture into a shallow casserole.**

**Arrange broccoli spears on top of rice-celery mixture with stems toward the center of the casserole.**

# Spanish Pork & Rice

*A hearty main dish with a Mediterranean background.*

1 tablespoon vegetable oil
4 lean pork chops
1/4 cup diced onion
1/3 cup diced celery
2 tablespoons diced green pepper
1 (1-lb.) can tomatoes

1-1/2 teaspoons salt
1/4 teaspoon pepper
2 cups *cooked* UNCLE BEN'S®
   CONVERTED® Brand Rice
2 tablespoons minced parsley

In a skillet, heat oil. Add chops. Brown on both sides. Remove chops. Add onion, celery and green pepper to drippings. Sauté until tender. Add tomatoes, salt and pepper. Top each chop with mound of 1/2 cup cooked rice. Pour tomato mixture over all. Sprinkle with parsley. Cover and refrigerate until ready to use.

Before serving bake, covered, at 350°F (177°C) for approximately 1 hour and 15 minutes. Makes 4 servings.

# Meatballs in Tomato Sauce

*You'll make this popular dish often.*

1 cup UNCLE BEN'S® Brown Rice
2-2/3 cups water
1 teaspoon salt
1 tablespoon butter or margarine
2 lbs. lean ground beef
1/2 cup finely chopped onion

2 tablespoons chopped parsley
2 teaspoons salt
1/2 teaspoon oregano
1 egg
1 (8-oz.) can tomato sauce

Cook rice with water, 1 teaspoon salt and butter or margarine according to package directions. Cool to room temperature. In a large bowl, combine rice, beef, onion, parsley, 2 teaspoons salt, oregano and egg. Mix well. Mixture will be soft. Shape into 16 to 18 balls. Place in a shallow 2-quart casserole. Pour tomato sauce over meat balls. Cover tightly and refrigerate until ready to use.

Before serving, bake at 400°F (205°C) about 55 minutes. Uncover and return to oven to thicken sauce, 5 to 10 minutes. Makes 6 to 8 servings.

# Brown Rice & Beef

*A fantastic dish with an unusual blend of spices*

1 cup UNCLE BEN'S® Brown Rice
2-2/3 cups water
1 teaspoon salt
1 tablespoon butter or margarine
1 tablespoon vegetable oil
1-1/2 lbs. ground beef
1 cup sliced celery
1/2 cup chopped onion

1 tablespoon flour
2 teaspoons salt
1/2 teaspoon dry mustard
1/8 teaspoon cinnamon
1/4 cup catsup
1/2 cup water
1 cup shredded mild Cheddar cheese

Cook rice with 2-2/3 cups water, 1 teaspoon salt and butter or margarine according to package directions. In a skillet, heat oil. Add ground beef and cook, stirring often, until meat is crumbly. Drain off excess fat. Add celery and onion. Cook until onion is tender, not brown. Blend in flour, salt, mustard and cinnamon. Add catsup and water; mix well. Stir in cooked brown rice and 2/3 cup of the cheese. Spoon into a 2-quart casserole. Cover and refrigerate until ready to use.

Before serving, bake at 375°F (191°C) until hot, about 40 to 45 minutes. Sprinkle with remaining cheese. Return to oven to melt cheese. Makes 6 servings.

# Crabmeat With Artichoke Hearts

*Serve this at your next gala affair.*

1 (6-1/4-oz.) pkg. UNCLE BEN'S®
  Fast Cooking Long Grain & Wild Rice
2 cups water
2 tablespoons butter or margarine
2 tablespoons butter or margarine
2 cups sliced fresh mushrooms
2 tablespoons butter or margarine
1/3 cup chopped onion
1/3 cup flour

1 cup half and half
1 cup chicken broth
3 tablespoons dry sherry
1 teaspoon salt
1/2 teaspoon basil
Dash of pepper
2 (6-oz.) pkgs. frozen crabmeat, thawed
1 (9-oz.) pkg. frozen artichoke hearts, thawed
1 cup shredded Swiss cheese

Lightly butter a 12" x 8" baking dish. Cook contents of rice and seasoning packets with water and 2 tablespoons butter or margarine according to package directions. In a medium saucepan, melt the second 2 tablespoons of butter or margarine. Add mushrooms and sauté lightly. Using a slotted spoon, transfer mushrooms to a small bowl and set aside. Add the third 2 tablespoons butter or margarine to saucepan; add onion. Cook until tender, not brown. Stir in flour. Add half and half and chicken broth. Cook until thick and smooth, stirring constantly. Stir in sherry, salt, basil and pepper. Combine rice, half and half mixture, mushrooms and 1/2 the crabmeat. Turn into buttered baking dish. Top with artichoke hearts and remaining crabmeat. Sprinkle cheese over top. Cover and refrigerate until ready to serve.

Before serving, bake at 425°F (218°C) until hot and bubbly, about 30 minutes. Makes 6 to 8 servings.

# Desserts

Rice seems like an old-fashioned dessert treat. Here are some brand-new dessert ideas from UNCLE BEN'S® kitchen. In these desserts, CONVERTED® Brand Rice remains firm and its separate, distinct grains add to the rich texture. Patio Dessert is a sweet fruit and rice blend. You can assemble Easy Cherry Delight in minutes. But the dessert spotlight is on spectacular but easy-to-prepare rice molds. Rice Pudding Mold With Cranberry-Rum Sauce is brightly colored, unusual and delicious. Or try Peaches-in-Rice Mold covered with luscious Apricot Sauce. Rice molds are impressive looking, sweet, cold and refreshing—a unique finale to your dinner.

*"Just Desserts" Party*
* Peaches-in-Rice Mold
  Pecan Pie
  Banana Cake
  Assorted Cookies

*Dinner's Special, So's Dessert*
  Roast Sirloin of Beef
  Yorkshire Pudding
  Puree of Broccoli
  Tender Cooked Baby Carrots
* Sacramento Parfait

*I'll Bring Dessert*
* Easy Cherry Delight

*Anytime Family Celebration*
  Turkey with Stuffing
  Cauliflower Au Gratin
  Raw Zucchini, Carrot &
  Celery Sticks
  Sliced Tomatoes
  Rolls
* Patio Dessert

*Salute to Spring*
  Broiled Lemon Chicken
  STUFF 'n SUCH in Tomato Cups
  Asparagus
* Springtime Rice Mold

*These recipes are in this section.*

# Peaches-in-Rice Mold

*Fresh peaches in a rich, elegant mold, covered with thick apricot sauce.*

1 cup UNCLE BEN'S® CONVERTED®
   Brand Rice
2-1/2 cups water
1 teaspoon salt
1/2 cup sugar
1/4 cup butter or margarine

1 cup whipping cream (1/2 pt.)
4 egg yolks, slightly beaten
1-1/2 teaspoons vanilla extract
1/2 teaspoon grated lemon peel
Lemony Peaches, see below
Apricot Sauce, see below

*Lemony Peaches:*
2 cups sugar
1 cup water

Juice and peel of 1 lemon
6 to 8 small ripe peaches

*Apricot Sauce:*
1-1/2 cups apricot preserves
1/4 cup water

1/4 cup kirsch or Grand Marnier liqueur

Oil a 1-quart ring mold. Combine rice, water, salt, sugar and butter or margarine in a large saucepan. Bring to a boil. Cover tightly. Simmer 20 minutes. Remove from heat. Let stand, covered, until all liquid is absorbed, about 5 minutes. Place whipping cream in a large, heavy skillet. Bring to a boil and boil about 2 minutes or until cream is reduced to 1/2 cup. Pour over egg yolks, stirring constantly. Stir egg-yolk-cream mixture into rice. Stir in vanilla and lemon peel. Pack into oiled ring mold. Chill 3 to 4 hours. To serve, invert to unmold onto a large serving plate. Drain syrup from Lemony Peaches and arrange them in the center of the rice mold. Pour Apricot Sauce over and serve at once. Makes 6 to 8 servings.

**Lemony Peaches:**
In a large saucepan, combine sugar, water, lemon juice and peel. Cook until the sugar dissolves. Add peaches. Simmer, partially covered for 12 to 15 minutes. Remove from heat and allow the peaches to cool in the syrup. Peel the peaches and return them to syrup. Cover and refrigerate.

**Apricot Sauce:**
In a small saucepan, heat apricot preserves and water over low heat. With a wooden spoon, press the preserves through a fine sieve into a small bowl and stir in the kirsch or Grand Marnier liqueur.

**Variation:**
If fresh peaches are not available, substitute chilled canned peach halves.

# Strawberry-Marble Rice Pudding

*Sweet and tart.*

1/2 cup UNCLE BEN'S® CONVERTED® Brand Rice
1-1/3 cups water
1/2 teaspoon salt
1/2 tablespoon butter or margarine

1 (10-oz.) pkg. frozen sweetened strawberries, thawed
1 (8-oz.) carton plain yogurt
3 to 4 tablespoons sugar
1 cup whipping cream, whipped

Chill 6 to 8 dessert dishes. Cook rice with water, salt and butter or margarine according to package directions for half the basic recipe. Chill. Drain strawberries well; reserve juice. Fold strawberries, yogurt and sugar into whipped cream. Fold in chilled rice. Spoon into dessert dishes. Chill. Just before serving, drizzle strawberry juice around edges of desserts. Makes 6 servings.

# Rice Pudding Mold With Cranberry-Rum Sauce

*Ladle bright Cranberry-Rum Sauce over this unusual dessert.*

1/2 cup UNCLE BEN'S® CONVERTED® Brand Rice
1-1/3 cups water
1/2 teaspoon salt
1 envelope (1 tablespoon) unflavored gelatin
1/2 cup kirsch liqueur

1 (8-oz.) can whole-cranberry sauce
2 eggs, separated
1/4 cup sugar
1/2 cup chopped pecans
1 cup whipping cream (1/2 pt.)
1/4 cup sugar
Cranberry-Rum Sauce, see below

*Cranberry-Rum Sauce:*

2 cups fresh cranberries
1/2 cup pineapple juice
3/4 cup sugar
1 teaspoon shredded orange peel

1/2 teaspoon shredded lemon peel
1/4 cup light rum
2 tablespoons butter or margarine
1/4 teaspoon salt

Oil a 6-cup mold. Cook rice with water and salt according to package directions for half the basic recipe, omitting butter. In a large saucepan, combine gelatin, kirsch liqueur and cranberry sauce. Heat over low heat until gelatin is dissolved. Stir in cooked rice. Beat egg yolks and 1/4 cup sugar until thick and lemon-colored. Stir small amount of rice-cranberry mixture into yolks. Stir back into rice-cranberry mixture. Cook over low heat until slightly thickened, stirring constantly, 2 to 3 minutes. Fold in pecans. Chill until mixture mounds. Beat whipped cream until stiff. Beat egg whites until frothy. Add remaining 1/4 cup sugar gradually, beating constantly until egg whites form stiff peaks. Fold beaten egg whites and whipped cream into rice-cranberry mixture. Turn into mold. Chill until set. Invert to unmold. Serve with Cranberry-Rum Sauce. Makes 8 servings.

Cranberry-Rum Sauce:

In a medium saucepan, combine cranberries, pineapple juice, sugar, orange peel and lemon peel. Bring to a boil and cover. Simmer until cranberries are tender, about 10 minutes. Remove from heat. Stir in rum, butter or margarine and salt. Makes 2 cups of sauce.

**Rice-Pudding Mold With Cranberry-Rum Sauce**

# Patio Dessert

*An easy refrigerator-to-patio treat.*

2 cups UNCLE BEN'S® QUICK™
  Brand Rice
1-2/3 cups water
1/2 teaspoon salt
1 tablespoon butter or margarine
1 teaspoon vanilla

1 cup dairy sour cream
1/4 cup maple syrup or brown sugar,
  firmly packed
Green grapes, blueberries or strawberries,
  for garnish

Chill 6 dessert dishes. Cook rice with water, salt and butter or margarine according to package directions. Stir in vanilla. Cover and chill. Just before serving, fold in sour cream and maple syrup or brown sugar. Spoon into dessert dishes. Garnish with grapes or berries. Makes 6 servings.


# Sacramento Parfait

*Fruit, nuts and rice in a delectable parfait.*

1-1/2 cups *cooked* and chilled UNCLE BEN'S®
  CONVERTED® Brand Rice
1/2 cup seedless raisins
1 (8-3/4-oz.) can apricot halves,
  drained and halved
1/4 cup toasted chopped almonds

1/2 cup whipping cream
1/4 cup sugar
1/4 teaspoon ground cinnamon
1/4 teaspoon ground nutmeg
Maraschino cherries, if desired

In a large bowl, combine cooked rice, raisins, apricots and almonds. Mix. Combine whipping cream, sugar, cinnamon and nutmeg. Whip until cream forms firm peaks. Fold into rice mixture. Chill 4 to 6 hours. Spoon into dessert dishes or parfait glasses and top each with a maraschino cherry, if desired. Makes 6 servings.


# Fruit Treat

*Here's a dessert you can make a meal of!*

1 cup UNCLE BEN'S®
  Brown Rice
2-2/3 cups water
1 teaspoon salt
1 tablespoon butter or margarine
1/4 cup honey, or to taste

1/4 cup lemon juice
3 cups diced assorted fresh fruits and berries
2 oranges, peeled, diced and drained
1 large red unpeeled apple, chopped
1/2 cup chopped pecans
About 1/4 cup yogurt

Cook rice with water, salt and butter or margarine according to package directions. Chill thoroughly. In a large bowl, combine rice, honey and lemon juice. Mix well. Mix in fruits and pecans. Add yogurt as needed to bind ingredients together. Chill thoroughly. Makes 8 to 10 servings.

# Springtime Rice Mold

*Make this rum-flavored dessert ahead for a carefree dinner.*

1 pt. fresh strawberries
1/3 cup sugar
2 tablespoons lemon juice
Cold water
2 (3-oz.) pkgs. lemon gelatin
1 cup boiling water
1/4 cup rum

1 (2-oz.) pkg. dessert-topping mix
1/2 cup milk
1/2 teaspoon rum flavoring
4 cups *cooked* UNCLE BEN'S®
    QUICK™ Brand Rice
Fresh mint leaves, if desired

Oil a shallow 2-quart ring mold. Wash and hull strawberries; reserve a few for garnish. Cut remaining berries into quarters. Sprinkle with sugar and let stand 1 to 2 hours. Drain berries; reserve juice. Add lemon juice and cold water to strawberry juice to make 2-1/3 cups liquid. In a large bowl, dissolve lemon gelatin in boiling water. Add strawberry-lemon juice mixture and rum. Chill until partially set. Whip dessert-topping mix with milk and rum flavoring following directions on package. Fold into gelatin. Fold in cooked rice and quartered berries. Turn into mold and chill until set. Invert to unmold. Garnish with reserved whole berries and fresh mint leaves, if desired. Makes 12 servings.

# Rice Pudding With Sherry-Berry Topping

*An old favorite with a fancy twist.*

2 cups UNCLE BEN'S® QUICK™
    Brand Rice
1-2/3 cups water
1 tablespoon butter
Peel of 1 lemon, grated
1/2 teaspoon salt
2 (3-5/8-oz.) pkgs. vanilla-pudding and
    pie-filling mix

4 cups milk
1 pt. strawberries, washed and hulled
1/4 cup confectioners' sugar
2 to 3 tablespoons cream sherry
Strawberries and mint leaves for garnish,
    if desired

In a large saucepan, combine rice, water, butter, lemon peel and salt. Stir. Bring to a *vigorous* boil and cover. Turn heat down. Simmer until all liquid is absorbed, about 5 minutes. Chill. Combine pudding mix and milk and make pudding according to directions on package. Fold rice into pudding. Place berries, sugar and sherry into blender container and purée. Use as a topping for rice pudding. Garnish with additional strawberries and mint leaves, if desired. Makes 10 servings.

**Variations:**

Substitute 4 cups of any cooked vanilla pudding for the vanilla-pudding and pie-filling mix.

Substitute raspberries, blueberries or other fruit for strawberries.

Spoon Cream-Cheese Filling over baked, cooled crust.

Spread Rice Pudding over the chilled Cream-Cheese Filling. Chill until pudding is firm.

# How To Make Easy Cherry Delight

Spoon cherry-pie filling over the chilled pudding. Chill until served.

At serving time, chilled layers will slice neatly. Top each serving with non-dairy whipped topping.

# Easy Cherry Delight

*Crunchy pastry, filled with cream cheese, rice pudding and cherry topping. Mmmm.*

1 cup flour
1/2 cup butter or margarine
1 cup coarsely chopped pecans
Cream-Cheese Filling, see below

Rice Pudding, see below
1 (1-lb. 5-oz.) can cherry-pie filling
Non-dairy whipped topping for garnish

*Cream Cheese Filling:*
1 (8-oz.) pkg. cream cheese
1 cup non-dairy whipped topping

1 cup sifted confectioners' sugar

*Rice Pudding:*
1/2 cup UNCLE BEN'S® CONVERTED®
   Brand Rice
1-1/3 cups water
1/2 teaspoon salt

1/2 tablespoon butter or margarine
4 cups milk
2 (3-5/8-oz.) pkgs. vanilla instant-pudding mix

Preheat oven to 350°F (177°C). Lightly butter a 13" x 9" pan. Combine flour and butter or margarine in a bowl. Cut butter or margarine into flour with knives or pastry blender until mixture resembles fine crumbs. Add pecans and mix well. Press in an even layer into buttered pan. Bake until lightly browned, about 20 minutes. Cool. Spoon Cream-Cheese Filling over cooled crust. Spread Rice Pudding over Cream-Cheese Filling. Chill until firm. Spoon cherry-pie filling over pudding; chill. Just before serving garnish each serving with a dollop of non-dairy whipped topping. Makes 12 servings.

**Cream Cheese Filling:**
Beat cream cheese and non-dairy whipped topping until smooth. Add confectioners' sugar, stirring until free of lumps.

**Rice Pudding:**
Cook rice with water, salt and butter or margarine according to package directions for half the basic recipe. Cool. Whip milk and pudding mixes together until thickened. Fold in rice. Chill until firm.

# Index

**A**

Apple-Walnut Wild Rice, 65
Apricot Chicken Au Vin, 103
Apricot-Yogurt Bread, 23
Artichoke Hearts With Wild Rice, 52

**B**

Bacon-Lettuce-Tomato Rice, 74
Bacon-Vegetable Platter, 49
Baked Fish With Orange Stuffing, 118
Baked Lemon Pie, 171
Baked Pork Chops & Brown Rice, 89
Baked Rice & Cheese Italiano, 127
Baked Stroganoff Meatballs, 94
Banana-Curried Salad, 39
Barbecue Bonus Salad, 42
Beef & Cheese Crepes, 136
Beef Paprikash, 161
Beef & Rice Stroganoff, 154
Beef Rolls With Creamy Mushroom Sauce, 134-135
Beef & Snow Peas Chinese-Style, 84
Beef Strudel With Burgundy Mushroom Sauce, 83
Bengal Beef, 92
Bombay Bruffins, 25
Braised Rice-Stuffed Lamb, 125
Brandied Chicken Breasts, 101
Broccoli Bake With Wild Rice, 162-163
Broccoli-Cheese Casserole, 48
Broiled Steaks & Wild Rice, 84
Brown Rice Garden Salad, 32
Brown Rice & Beef, 165
Brown Rice Pilaf, 60
Burgundy Short Ribs With Chili Rice, 82

**C**

Calas, 18
Calcutta Casserole, 146
California Easy-Living Supper, 143
California-Style Beef Stew, 23
Calypso Chicken, 104
Camper's Rice Fry, 145
Cantonese Rice & Asparagus, 57
Cantonese-Style Beef & Green Beans, 94
Carmen Salad, 31
Cheese-Rice Bake, 66
Cheese-Spinach Casserole, 46
Chicken Casserole Véronique, 98
Chicken-Mozzarella Bake, 99

Chicken & Ham With Wild Rice, 96
Chicken Oriental, 99
Chicken Salad With Tarragon Vinaigrette, 43
Chili Salad in Cherry Tomatoes, 16-17
Chili & Sour Cream Salad, 31
Chinese Fried Rice, 68-69
Chinese Pepper Beef, 150
Cioppino, 14
Clams Mornay, 21
Cod Italiano, 118
Conversion To Metric Measure, 12
Cooking Methods, 8-10
Coq Au Bourguignon, 157
Cornish Hens With Wild Rice, 106
Coulibiac, 159
Crabmeat Enchiladas, 137
Crabmeat Salad Bites, 22
Crabmeat With Aritchoke Hearts, 165
Cranberried Duck With Wild Rice Stuffing, 138-139
Cranberry Stuffing en Casserole, 64
Creamed Onions in Wild Rice Ring, 56
Cream of Wild Rice Soup, 26
Creamy Curried Shrimp With Coconut Rice, 119
Creole Ham Supper, 143
Curried Apricot Pork With Pecan Rice, 130
Curried Buffet Meatballs, 130-131
Curried Chicken & Wild Rice Bake, 160
Curried Rice Balls, 26

**D**

Desserts, 166-174

**E**

Easy Cherry Delight, 172-173
Eggs-Carmen Brunch, 14
Emerald Rice, 69
Entertaining, 124-141

**F**

Facts About Uncle Ben's® Rice Products, 7
Fahrenheit to Celsius, 12
Fisherman's Wharf Casserole, 114
Fish Kebabs Wtih Pineapple Sauce, 114
Florentine Rice Ring, 47
Florentine Rice Roll, 20
Fresh Shrimp Risotto, 113
Fresh Vegetable Salad, 34
Fruit Treat, 170
Fruited Brown Rice, 61

# Index

Fruited Pork Chops, 78
Fruited Salad, 36-37

**G**
Gazpacho Salad, 30
Gazpacho Skillet, 148-149
Gourmet Stuffed Chicken Breasts, 103
Green Peppers Stuffed With Mediterranean Rice, 50-51
Green Rice Souffle, 48

**H**
Ham a la King With Pecan Rice, 161
Ham in Orange-Mustard Sauce, 81
Ham Loaf With Whipped Horseradish Sauce, 79
Ham & Rice Stuffed Tomatoes, 140
Ham Véronique, 141
Hearty Peach Salad, 37
Hearty Polish Soup, 15
Holiday Stuffing, 71
Honeyed Apples in Brown Rice, 61
Hot Chicken Salad, 35
How To Cook It, 8-10
How To Know When You Are Doing It Right, 11

**I**
Imperial Salad, 43
In-A-Hurry Pork & Zucchini Rice, 147
Islander's Lime Chicken, 110
Italian Chicken With Saffron Rice, 111

**K**
Kinds of Rice, 6

**L**
Lamb Chops & Rice Niçoise, 86-87
Lamb Chops With Lemony Wild Rice, 86
Lamb Curry Calcutta, 93
Lamb Mesheke, 133
Lovin' Rice Salad, 38

**M**
Make Ahead, 156-165
Meal-In-One Salad, 41
Meatballs in Tomato Sauce, 164
Meats, 76-94
Mediterranean Beef & Artichokes, 151
Mediterranean Ham Buffet, 140
Metric Conversions, 12
Mexican Arroz con Pollo, 109
Mexican Fire & Ice Casserole, 74
Mexican Fruited Chicken, 107
Mile-High Treasure Pie, 132

Minted Lamb Supreme, 82
Mixed-Vegetable Curry, 45
Monterey Brown Rice, 70
Monterey Risotto, 71

**N**
Napa Valley Chicken, 97
Natural-Goodness Bread, 19
Niçoise Rice Salad, 35
Nutrition Information, 4-5

**O**
Onion Brown Rice With Carrots, 46
Onion-Fried Chicken and Wild Rice, 158
Orange-Glazed Chicken & Peaches, 110
Orange Holiday Rice, 73
Oriental Chicken-Cucumber Sauté, 155
Oriental Quiche, 141
Oriental Wild Rice, 75

**P**
Paella, 128-129
Patio Dessert, 170
Peaches-in-Rice Mold, 167
Persian Rice, 67
Pimiento-Cheese Party Ball, 27
Plum-Glazed Chicken, 108-109
Plum-Glazed Duckling, Apricot Rice, 97
Polynesian Ham Salad, 42
Polynesian Orange Rice, 67
Pork Adobo, 77
Pork Chops California-Style, 90
Pork Chops Rio Grande, 90-91
Pork Chops Veracruz, 85
Pork-Pear Casserole, 89
Pork Tenderloin Jardiniere, 77
Poultry, 95-111
Provencale Beef, 158

**Q**
Quick Ham Dinner, 147
Quick Paella, 151
Quick Skillet Dishes, 142-155
Quick Taco Skillet, 145

**R**
Rainbow Trout With Mushroom Stuffing, 123
Raisin Rice, 66
Ratatouille Rice Cups, 47
Red Beans & Rice, 70
Reuben Croquettes, 81

# Index

Rice a la Grecque, 75
Rice & Rye Bread, 15
Rice Pudding Mold With Cranberry-Rum Sauce, 168-169
Rice Pudding With Sherry-Berry Topping, 171
Rice—The World's Most Important Food, 2-3
Risi e Bisi, 72-73

**S**
Sacramento Parfait, 170
Salad Appetizers, 28
Salad Roll-ups, 40-41
Salads, 29-43
Sausage-Apricot Pastry Logs, 132
Sausage & Rice, 143
Savory Chicken Kiev With Pecan Wild Rice, 160
Scallops With Carnival Rice, 115
Scallops & Wild Rice, 122
Scallops With Glazed Walnuts, 113
Scampi Rice, 119
Seafood, 112-123
Seafood Jambalaya, 127
Seafood Salad With Orange Vinaigrette, 30
Seasonal-Fruit Salad, 32-33
Seasoning packets, 7
Sherried Chinese Chicken, 107
Sherried Chinese Chicken, 107
Sherried-Mushroom Wild Rice, 65
Sherried Pea Bisque, 21
Shish Kebabs With Mint Rice, 88
Short Ribs Italian-Style, 93
Side Dishes, 59-75
Sole Roll-Ups With Sweet-Sour Sauce, 116-117
South Seas Rice & Snow Peas, 55
Southwestern Rice, 64
Spanish Pork & Rice, 164
Spanish Rice, 45
Specialties, 13-28
Specialty of the House, 38
Spectacular Appetizer, 28
Spiced Chicken 106
Spinach-Broccoli Casserole, 52
Spinach & Brown Rice Greek-Style, 55
Spinach Salad With Oriental Vinaigrette, 34
Spring Pork With Rice Loaf, 79
Springtime Rice Mold, 171
Stir-Fry Chicken & Pea Pods, 152-153
Stir-Fry Ham & Peaches, 146

Stir-Fry Shrimp & Wild Rice, 115
Strawberry-Marble Rice Pudding, 168
Stuffed Artichokes With Lemon Butter, 54-55
Stuffed Cabbage, 137
Stuffed Grape Leaves, 16-17
Stuffed Pepper Appetizers, 22
Surf & Turf Rice, 126
Surprise Pie, 92
Sweet & Pungent Chicken & Rice, 96
Sweet & Sour Pork, 144
Sweet & Sour Shrimp, 120-121
Sweet & Sour Tuna Salad, 39
Swiss-Sausage Rice, 155

**T**
Taco Soup, 27
Tangerine Chicken, 102
Tex-Mex Chili, 145
Thursday's Wild Beef & Vegetable Loaf, 78
Toasted Almond Rice, 60
Tomato-Okra Pilaf, 53
Tomato-Rice Quiche, 18
Tomato-Rice Ring Italian-Style, 62-63
Tuna Creole Skillet, 122
Tuna Supper, 150
Turkey-Almond Custard, 104

**U**
Uncle Ben's Ragoût, 149

**V**
Valencia Rice & Carrots, 56
Veal Marsala With Risotto, 85
Veal & Orange Skillet Dinner, 154
Vegetable-Nut Patties, 53
Vegetable-Rice Ring, 125
Vegetables, 44-58

**W**
West Indian Chicken Curry, 100-101
Wild Rice Mushrooms, 19
Wild Rice Oyster Bake, 123

**Z**
Zesty Chicken & Rice, 111
Zucchini Appetizers, 24-25
Zucchini With Brown Rice Stuffing, 58

9.237581242